Everyman's Search

Everyman's Search

by
Rebecca Beard

Published by
ARTHUR JAMES LIMITED
The Drift, Evesham, Worcs.

"The Drift is God's Gift"

© Stella Wheeler 1969.

First Published in England May 1951
Reprinted September 1951
Reprinted November 1951
Reprinted December 1951
Reprinted December 1952
Reprinted July 1954
Reprinted April 1956
Reprinted October 1957
Reprinted July 1960
Reprinted June 1962
Reprinted March 1965
Reprinted October 1969
Reprinted September 1972

ISBN : 0 85305 053 8

131.

ACKNOWLEDGMENTS

The author and publisher wish to acknowledge the following
sources from which quotations have been used, with the permission
of the publisher :

Mind and Body by Dr. Flanders Dunbar. Random House, Inc., New
York. Copyright 1947.

Human Destiny by Lecomte du Nuoy. Longmans, Green & Co., Inc.,
New York. Copyright 1947.

MADE AND PRINTED IN GREAT BRITAIN BY PURNELL AND SONS, LTD.
PAULTON (SOMERSET) AND LONDON

To

ANNE, LUCILLE and CASSANDRA

The
BISHOP OF CROYDON

says:

Here is a book which is not merely interesting but of outstanding significance. I believe that it is one of *the most important books that has ever been written on the subject of Spiritual Healing*.

The writer, an American doctor, shows in her thesis the striking influence of the mind over the body. She stresses the importance of positive thinking and expectant prayer.

The author has herself been healed of serious heart trouble by a deep faith in God and by prayer—she is now actively engaged in psycho-somatic healing.

She has some remarkable things to say about the cause of accidents, stating that many accidents are caused by emotional disorder. She claims that diseases like diabetes, arthritis, and angina pectoris can be greatly relieved if not entirely cured by faith and prayer.

She also submits a very remarkable story of the complete healing of an advanced case of cancer.

This is a book which should be read by every priest and by any layman who is keen to help his fellow-men. The book ends with a few admirable suggestions for meditation.

8th February, 1951.   *Cuthbert Croydon**

* Since writing this Foreword, the Bishop of Croydon has become the Bishop of Coventry.

CONTENTS

Materia Medica to Spiritual Therapy

Each man in searching travels his own road, yet his experience can be of value to other seekers.

Our experience led us from materia medica to spiritual therapy. This might seem, at first sight, to be more in the nature of a conversion than a transition, yet as I look back upon the steps over which we came it seems an inevitable transition for one trained in the scientific field, if that one be willing to go far enough. Whether one advances along this road or not depends, it seems to me, upon a willingness to explore with an open mind.

In my earlier years, science was my religion. I was so fascinated and enthralled by the things I was learning that I was open to nothing else. I owe much to science and to my training in science, for my first deep concept of God came to me through my introduction to the laws of valence, the atomic theory and the periodic system. All these revealed to me the underlying order and rationality of nature and gave me an awareness of the dependability and unchangeableness of natural law which is still the foundation of my enlarging faith.

It is not easy to tell you the steps in the transition from materia medica to spiritual therapy. It is a matter of picking up threads and weaving them together, as one recalls them. Often the things that have motivated us become vague as time goes on. It is difficult to recall just what the actual steps were, but as nearly as I can I shall give them to you, because if one is searching for a path it is sometimes a help to know of the path over which another has travelled.

Early in my hospital work I had charge of the drug-room because I had a steady hand and could pour from one bottle to another without spilling. Each morning we filled the bottles for the wards out of the stock-bottles in the drug-room. After some months of this I found there was something strange about the popularity of drugs and the faith of the doctors in certain preparations. One drug would appear on the horizon and would be acclaimed by all the doctors. It was difficult to keep the bottles filled because of the demand. Then, little by little, doubts and criticism would creep in, the negative reports would be heard, until that drug lost its popularity. The huge bottles out of which the others were filled were gradually pushed further and further back on the shelf, and I said to myself, "Isn't that queer? Why?"

Today the medical world seems to be moving out of the world of drugs, as such, into the use of natural remedies which are more or less native to the body. Many have come into the recognition of hormones and enzymes, vitamins and minerals, all of which the body itself would appropriate or produce if it was always operating in perfect harmony.

Another thing happened once in a while which made me ask, "Why?" A patient in the hospital in an extremely serious condition from exhaustion or shock might pass into a coma, and we could scarcely catch the heart-beat or the respiration. We would send out a frantic search for the doctor in charge of the case. Perhaps he could not quickly be located, and we would be at the bedside, tense with anxiety.

You learn to know the sound of different doctors as they come into a hospital, so as we stood there at the bed, with our fingers on the patient's pulse, we would sense, rather than hear, the grapevine message that would pass along the corridors, "The doctor has come." "The doctor is here."

How the patient would be aware of it is still a mystery, but before he could even come up the steps the patient would breathe a great sigh of relief and begin to relax. We could feel the pulse coming back, and the respiration deepening. We could feel the warmth of new life flowing through the body, and see the colour return slowly to the lips and ears. "The doctor is here!" Sometimes the release from fear would be so marked that one could not help realizing that here was something more than met the eye.

Then, once in a while, there would be a consultation over someone who was very near death. The verdict would go out, "There is no hope. It is a matter of hours." The doctors might have agreed that nothing more could be done. Then possibly a pastor, a lovely mother, wife or friend would come and say to us, "May we go in? We would like to stay at the bedside." Always consent was given. The door would be closed. The nurses would go in only on call. We would walk quietly past that room, for we knew they were praying.

Once in a while, not always, but it happened, the patient who was not expected to live would get well and walk out of the hospital in a few days. The doctors, shrugging their shoulders, might say, "It is just one of those things." And I would ask myself again, "Why?" "Why don't they ask? If it could happen once why could it not happen again? What is it?" But no one asked. No one sought the answer. Today we feel it is definitely not "just one of those things", and a mere shrug of the shoulders is not going to carry it off.

Later, there came a time in my life when science and the love of scientific knowledge did not seem to answer the need. I think many of us who have been deeply impressed in our scientific training have, all unconsciously perhaps, an unawakened religious spirit. Anyone who reads Lecomte du Nuoy's books realizes that what he says is true, that a man of science without imagination is not a true scientist. He must be able to formulate an hypothesis, or he is only a tabulator of facts. He must have the divine imagination and power of visualization to step out on his supposition and prove it; so, also, must we be able to leap the gap from facts which are known to those facts which are but yet dimly discerned.

But so often we do not see or feel this thing until we are forced to our knees, and have come to the place where we can no longer go under our own limited human power and strength. I came to that place, and my colleagues who knew me well and loved me, said, "You must put your affairs in order, for you cannot live through another heart-attack."

When faced by that ultimatum you realize that you have nothing within yourself with which to meet it. For the first time in my life, literally and figuratively, I went down on my knees. It was only then that God became real, and I began to sense the great power that was outside of myself, and yet was part of me, and I cried, "If it is possible, take this from me. Either take it from me or take me. I have gone as far as I can."

A wonderful revelation came; a great spiritual illumination. I knew then that I was healed, and I knew that the rest of my life would be given to helping others find that healing. How, then, to get out of the field in which I was serving, and move into the other field in which I wanted to serve?

* * *

Long before this I had given up the use of drugs. They have their place. I do not imply anything against them. There are thousands of agencies, and they seem to me to be all God-given. They have their place and their use in some part of our process of growth, and we do not depreciate them. But when we learn that there is only one power behind all the agencies, and we choose to go directly to that power, then the agencies lose their importance, and we lose our dependence upon them and our need of them.

So there is no quarrel, ever, as to what you use. What you use simply determines how far you have gone. When you are ready to use only the power of God you will not need the agency. But that time should never be forced. One should hesitate to say, "I will give it up and see if I can do without it." You will see, beloved, but you may not see what you want to see, for faith must precede. The signs follow.

Late in 1945 Dr. Glenn Clark called a conference to be held near Minneapolis. He invited those who had been practising spiritual healing to meet with him with the hope that we might be able to pool our findings and share our experiences in healing through prayer. Each person who attended had done some outstanding work in the field of spiritual therapy. They represented a cross-section of religious and scientific groups, although none came as a direct representative of any group.

The spirit of the people whom I met at that first Healing Advance was beyond anything I had ever experienced. I had attended many medical conventions where everyone was stampeding and stepping on one another's heels, so anxious were they to be heard. Here were thirty-five or forty consecrated people with the light of God shining in their faces, every one of whom said, "I would rather not talk. I want so much to hear what you have discovered"—eager and willing they were to step aside.

We had heard of the "wonderful triumvirate", as Dr. Clark called them—Louise Eggleston, of Norfolk, Virginia, who had organized more prayer groups than any other woman in the country; Ruth Robison, whose husband was pastor of a Methodist Church; and Agnes Sanford, wife of an Episcopalian rector, and author of *The Healing Light*.

One after another these three remarkable women on that first afternoon told their stories of personal healing and of the healing of others through prayer. Dr. Stanley Tyler and I were the two doctors of medicine in the group, and I don't think either of us sat back in our chairs while they were talking.

It was immediately after this meeting that we all unwittingly re-enacted one of the miracles recorded in the New Testament. Dr. Tyler came out of the meeting that afternoon all afire. He had told us when he first came to the Advance of a patient who had had a stomach ulcer which perforated just before Dr. Tyler was due to leave for the conference. We knew he had been torn between his duty to stay with his patient and his desire to come to the Advance. Finally, he turned the patient over to his colleague and came, but the man was on his mind and heart for he knew he was desperately ill with peritonitis.

At this time Dr. Tyler was not so much interested in healing through prayer as he was in his new-found psychosomatic discoveries. He was full of his subject and eager to speak of it to his fellow townspeople but they seemed reluctant to listen.

When Agnes Sanford finished speaking on that first afternoon Dr. Tyler and the rest of us were all so moved that we left the room in silence.

*   *   *

In the recreation hall later Dr. Tyler came to us and said, "I know what I am going to do. I am going to take Agnes Sanford to my town and heal my patient and then those people will come to me and say, 'What's it all about, Doc?' and I will have a chance to tell my story."

Mrs. Sanford sat beside Dr. Tyler during this outburst, then she looked up at him with a smile and said, "Wait a minute. I am not in the habit of going out to heal people so that someone may have an opportunity to tell their story. We must take this under advice. We will pray over it."

To this the Doctor agreed.

The next morning we came down to the lodge before breakfast to warm ourselves by the fire, for the mornings were chilly. As Dr. Tyler came into the room Mrs. Sanford reached for her purse and remarked, "All right, Stanley, let's go." But Dr. Tyler said he would like to telephone first. "All right," Agnes Sanford replied. "We will have breakfast and after you have telephoned you can bring us your news."

We sat at the breakfast-table with our backs to the fireplace, facing the door, and as Dr. Tyler came in we knew something was wrong. Agnes and I both thought the worst had happened. Stanley came over to the table and burst out with, "Doggone, I knew we would wait too long!"

We both felt that this was rather a harsh way to break the news. Agnes was sympathetic. "I am so sorry, Stanley."

He looked at her with a bewildered expression and we were puzzled. "What do you mean?" he asked.

"Well," she countered, "didn't the man die? Isn't that what you were trying to tell us?"

"Doggone, no," he replied impatiently. "His wife answered the telephone and said he was all right. He got up this morning, ate his breakfast and is perfectly well." Dr. Tyler sounded like a small boy who has had his new boots taken away from him, and we could scarcely believe he was serious. But it was true. The man was healed and well, and Dr. Tyler did not know, and we did not realize until afterwards, that the centurion's story had been enacted in real life before us.

You will notice Stanley Tyler did not say, "IF she can heal him." He said, "I am going to take her down there and heal that man, and when he is healed the people will say to me, 'What is all this about?'" You see, there was absolutely no question in Stanley's mind. And in that self-same hour the man was healed! Dr. Stanley Tyler has been trying ever since to tell them what it is all about.

The following October, 1946, my husband and I both attended the second Healing Advance in Minneapolis, and in the spring of 1947 we gave up our home, and went to Merrybrook to start our work in spiritual therapy.

Hurdles

IN LOOKING back over the experiences of twenty years of medical practice we recalled this one and that one whom the doctors believed could live only a short time, and yet they lived, and some of them lived a very long time. The question of curable and incurable was, for us, the first hurdle.

A report issued by the Churches' Council of Healing, an inter-denominational body originated by the late Archbishop of Canterbury, William Temple, says that the Council deplores the frequent use by doctors of the word "incurable", continuing, "The Christian doctor is coming more and more to regard it as scientifically unsound to pronounce any illness incurable, and is recognizing the unseen factor of spiritual regeneration as his greatest ally."

When we came into the idea of meeting all sickness, all problems, with this one solution—prayer—we very naturally said, "What of these conditions which are called incurable? What of these diseases which so far science says cannot be healed?" The pronouncement of a condition as "incurable" was something I was no longer able to make because experience had continued to teach me that through the power of prayer such conditions were not always incurable. No longer was it possible for me to say to a patient, "You have not long to live. There is no hope." How could anyone know?

As time went on I found myself more and more reluctant not only to make a definite prognosis of a patient's condition, but to make a diagnosis, because I realized that by saying to a person, "You have a serious disorder, or a definitely diseased organ," I was implanting into their subconscious mind a positive picture which was going to be difficult for them to forget or to ignore.

The transition from materia medica to spiritual therapy was not one of giving up the use of drugs. I had not used them for a long time, unless one classes the native remedies like hormones and vitamins as drugs. The hurdle I could not get over was this one of diagnosis. When a physician no longer makes diagnoses he no longer practises.

Then there arose the question of whether or not it is right to heal anyone through prayer. The right of physical science to try any method which promises a return to health is never questioned. Why, then, should there be a question about healing through spiritual power alone? Do we say to the surgeon or to the doctor, "Do you think it is right to heal this person?" We could not understand why we should hesitate to heal through spiritual means.

Lewis MacLachlan in his book, *Intelligent Prayer,* has a good deal to say on this subject. "Belief that disease can be and ought to be healed by prayer is often vigorously and sometimes indignantly resisted. The objection is not to healing, but to faith healing. People submit to hazardous experiments of all kinds, but cannot believe God will heal them in any other way. . . . Like Naaman, they take offence at the very simplicity of faith. They believe in healing but only by material means. They expect God to heal them, but only in ways of man's own choosing! Faith has been transferred from spiritual to material forces. . . . We have gained so much knowledge about material things we have lost much of our even more precious knowledge of spiritual things.

"We live in an ordered universe where the divine power is manifested in the operation of natural law. . . . When we pray for health and healing, we are appealing to the laws of God's ordered universe."

*　　*　　*

The next hurdle was a common one. It was the question of functional and organic conditions. Many people believe that prayer could be effective in functional disorders, but resist the belief that prayer can meet an organic change. The clarification of this point we made a subject of earnest prayer, and there seemed to come to us a direct answer in the words of a great scientist, Virchow, who did his greatest research work at the end of the last century. His words came back and back into my consciousness. They were these, "The cells that we find in the body in disease are exactly the same cells that we find in health, only altered in their appearance."

A pathologist looking through the microscope at a slide can tell by the appearance of the cells the pathological changes that have taken place in them, recognizing certain disease patterns. It is not a foreign cell which has usurped the place of a healthy cell. It is the identical cell of the healthy body, altered in appearance. On the other hand, a functional disorder is simply the inability of a cell to do its work. The function of the part is disturbed first, then gradually the changes take place in the cell itself, and we term this organic.

Think of yourself for a moment as an individual cell in the body. Suppose something were to happen to you during the next few months which would put you in an unnatural situation so that you were overburdened with problems, overworked, undernourished, and discouraged. At first your work would suffer. This would be a functional disorder. At the end of six months or a year you would not look the same. Your appearance might be so greatly altered that people would not easily recognize you, yet you would be the same person, wouldn't you? You would have all the possibilities of coming back to your natural state if the conditions were changed for the better.

It is difficult to draw a line between functional and organic, so we decided to consider them together, one having progressed further than the other. But we realized that, unwittingly, we put a strain on the cells of our bodies at times, and in our ignorance we hurt them badly. When through our words or by the power of our thoughts we suggest that they are weak, inefficient and inadequate, they become discouraged and listless. How would you respond to such suggestions made repeatedly? By being strong or weak? By manifesting health or disease? Would such constant criticism tend to make you feel happy and free, and enable you to do your work with joy and competency?

Since it is the same cell in health as in disease, only altered in function or appearance, then it is my belief that it will come back normally and naturally to a healthy condition when fed a proper mental diet.

Albert E. Cliffe, now famous Canadian chemist, has this to say about mental diet in his book, *Lessons in Living,* "For the past decade the whole world has been increasingly food conscious, with our leading magazines and journals publishing many articles on nutrition by specialists, most of them advising us to eat the foods we ought to eat instead of the foods we like to eat. The word vitamin is flung at us from every conceivable angle, with warnings of the dreadful things that will happen to us should we not heed their importance.

"As a food chemist, I know that the foods I eat each day are converted into the various parts of my body; in other words, my physical well-being depends for its development upon my daily diet. However, several years ago it was found that in spite of a so-called perfect diet of the right foods, many people suffered from disease, which according to the principles of nutrition should never have occurred.

"It was then that I came into my study of the mind, which has taught me that the food I give to my mind each hour and each day is of far greater importance than the food I give to my stomach. The words of Jesus in this respect are most applicable, 'Be not therefore anxious What shall we eat? or, What shall we drink?' By an application of His words I discovered that I alone was the cause of my intense suffering from stomach ulcers for twenty-seven years. Once I proved that my mental vitamins were the real source of my sickness or health, I became as I wished to become, healthy, happy and successful."

* * *

Then we came to the great hurdle—the headless horseman— that frightening thing which still holds the majority of the people of the world in the grip of fear—cancer. Our thought was—perhaps we can do everything through prayer but this, and yet, in our intuitive knowing we realized we dared not step out into the world of spiritual healing until we were absolutely sure that there was no barrier, and no hurdle that could not be overcome through God's healing power.

Because we had seen so many cancer sufferers we found this a tremendous hurdle to pass. We needed conviction, and we prayed, "Father, show us a condition that is unquestioned, about which no one can rationalize. We want to see something that is so evident in its outward manifestation that everyone can see it. We want to see something that is called incurable. We want to see an instantaneous healing, and we want to see it complete and made possible without any agency but prayer."

The answer to our prayer was the healing of our friend, Alice Newton, of Leavenworth, Kansas. It was not many weeks after we had prayed that she came to us in St. Louis. She had known me in Kansas City when I practised there. This is what she said, "I come because I have faith in you, and because I know you have something beyond medicine. I am in great need. Tell me the truth." Her appearance when we first saw her shocked us. Her huge abdomen was larger than a woman at full term pregnancy. She had the dreaded cachexia. Her emaciated body was scarcely able to carry the great burden. Her question was, "Do you think that I can be healed with prayer and nothing else?" For just a moment I felt a sinking feeling. "This is it," I thought. "You have asked for it. You wanted it."

You see, I did believe with my conscious mind, but my subconscious said, "Help Thou mine unbelief." Then I heard myself saying, "Yes, Alice, I believe. But I want to see it. I need to see it." "All right," she replied, "I'll do it for you and for my husband. I will go home and map out a programme and a schedule. I will follow it every day, and I have absolute faith now that our prayer will be answered, and the Lord will heal me."

She went home, cancelled all social obligations, did simple

things about the house, rested, walked in the open air, read her Bible, sang hymns, and prayed.

Every day she repeated the same pattern. She wrote to us often and in none of her letters did she ever suggest failure. She confidently awaited the moment of her healing. You have no idea how this strengthened our faith. The unswerving faith of one person is a tremendous factor in building the certainty of God's power in their lives. "Nor knowest thou what argument thine own life to thy neighbour's creed hath lent."

Among Alice's friends was a wonderful doctor who visited her often, not as a doctor but as a friend. His medical knowledge made him insist that she permit him to tap her. It was curious, but the relationship of doctor and patient seemed to be reversed between them. It was she who would say to him, "Don't you worry about me, Doctor." She often consoled and encouraged him, but he would go on his way, sorry and unbelieving. A spiritual conviction and certainty such as hers is not easily gained. It is necessary to pay the price. Her constancy of purpose lasted over a period of two years. Finally, one night, with no special preparation, the miracle happened.

At the time, her husband, a warder at the Leavenworth prison, was working from midnight until early morning. Alice retired shortly after he left for work, and went to sleep as usual. As she slept she had a vision of the disciples asleep as Jesus came down the mountainside from his lone vigil of prayer. His face was full of sorrow as he looked at the sleeping men, then he glanced over and smiled at her. Immediately the scene changed. It was the day of the crucifixion. The cross was being lowered into the hole that had been dug for it, the Master's body already nailed upon it. Torn with the thought of how the jar would hurt Him, she cried out, "Oh my Jesus," putting up her hand to steady His body and ease the suffering. At that moment her hand dropped to her abdomen and she awoke.

Turning on the light she saw that it was three o'clock. Only then she realized that her abdomen was perfectly flat.

The huge accumulation was gone! Immediately she felt all around her for moisture, thinking surely something had passed, but the bed was dry. There was no pain. Her spirit rejoiced, and she knew something wonderful had happened. So she turned out the light and waited.

* * *

Her husband came home rather early that morning. He felt, somehow, that something had happened. His excitement was so great when he heard the news that, to relieve him, she asked him to go for her friend, the doctor, cautioning him not to tell. Alice was a woman with a marvellous sense of humour, so before the doctor came she slipped a pillow under the bed-covers. She wanted to hear him scold. As he came in and stood at the foot of her bed, he shook a warning finger, saying, "Alice, I told you to let me tap you." She only smiled at first, then she said, "Yes, Doctor, and I told you that God was going to take care of me. See what He has done," and she pulled the pillow out and dropped it to the floor.

The doctor was speechless for a moment, then he rushed around the bed and knelt at her side. His questions came short and fast in his excitement. "What passed?" "What came away?" "Was there water?" "Was there blood?" "Did you perspire heavily?" "What was it?" To all she answered truthfully, "Nothing." Finally his questions ceased, for her answers continued to be, "No, nothing passed—nothing came away."

At last he said quietly, "No one but God could perform a miracle like that."

She stayed in bed for a week because they thought it was wise. People passed through the house constantly to see her in the days that followed. At the end of the week she was weighed, and it was found that she had lost thirty-eight-and-a-half pounds! That had disappeared overnight. And that was the answer to our prayer. That was a condition which no one could say had not existed. It could not be rationalized away. It was an instantaneous healing. No one could explain it. Where did thirty-eight-and-a-half pounds of actual weight go in three hours? That was the miracle. I had wanted to see something which I could not explain. God had answered my prayer.

Later, Alice came to St. Louis and asked if I wished to examine her. This I did, and found every organ fresh and virginal as though she had never been ill. She lives today. This happening has had a strange sequel. During the past twelve years the Leavenworth newspaper and the *Kansas City Star* have mentioned this remarkable recovery each January on the anniversary of Alice's healing!

Talking to Your Cells

As we are cells in the body of Christ, all of us together united and integrated in an organ of Christ, so in our bodies every tiny cell is an individual unit, living an individual life; each speck of protoplasm living its own life, separate from every other one, but united in perfect unity in the instinctive intelligence which rules everything in the body.

The cells of a certain organ have a definite appearance, so that the physiologist can, under the microscope, immediately recognize a bone cell, a gland cell, a muscle cell, and so on. He can recognize the cells even when they are changed in appearance. Now these cells lie bathed in a sea of lymph. When the blood is brought with all its nutrition and its oxygen through the blood-vessels and comes to the end of the last tiny capillary, the whole cargo is dumped into the sea of lymph.

It is as if each one of us lived in a boat on a vast ocean, and each one had to reach out from his boat and pick from the sea the food, the elements, the oxygen which he needed for his life, and the ingredients which he needed for his work; and then dump back into the sea of lymph all the debris and waste. Magnified astronomically this is the picture of the little cells and their life. Each one must take from the lymph the food he needs, the oxygen he must have, and the materials out of which he is to manufacture the particular secretion or substance he is to make. We marvel at the instinctive intelligence of the cells. Truly, as the Psalmist sang, "We are fearfully and wonderfully made."

The cells in the middle ear know how to take out ingredients that make ear-wax. The cells in the stomach walls know how to extract material to make hydrochloric acid. Others like the gland cells know how to take their ingredients from the same lymph deposit to manufacture the highly potent hormones. This is intelligence, but it is intuitive intelligence. It is not reasoning intelligence.

Sometimes I have found it easy to describe what goes on in the body by making a picture of a submarine. Let us think of our cells as the men in a submarine. They obey orders implicitly. The captain of the submarine is the only one who can look through the periscope and see the outside world. The men in the submarine must take the captain's word for the conditions in that outside world. They cannot see for themselves. They must act upon what he tells them.

You, the reasoning you, are the captain of your body. The men in the submarine are your cells. They cannot see outside. They must accept your word implicitly. You are the only one who can look through the periscope. So, some morning, like the captain of the submarine, you look out and send back a report of the conditions in the world about you, as you see them. You send the word down to the men below: "All fog. All mist. Nothing clear. Icebergs ahead. Danger all around." That is equivalent to saying, "Everything is going wrong," "I can't see my way out," "Everything seems to be against me," "Obstacles meet me at every turn," "The world is going to the dogs."

How would you feel if you were one of the men down in the submarine? You would put your head in your hands and say, "What's the use of washing the dishes and cleaning the galley? What's the use of cooking the food? Why keep up the daily regime?" Can you see the cells of your stomach which are at work down there trying to digest your food? You often discourage them with your words. You feed them on a diet of frustration and fear and blame them for not being efficient. Then suddenly one day you look through the periscope and say, "The sun is out. The fog is gone. No more icebergs visible. Full speed ahead." And the men down there breathe a sigh of relief. The danger is over. "Let's go to work. My, we have a lot to do. We have to clean this place, wash up all these dishes, and get rid of this collected waste." They sing for joy. When you get up tomorrow morning are you going to see sunshine or fog? Are you going to send joy to your cells or are you going to paralyse them with fear?

Dr. Binger says that man complains of his stomach, but truly the stomach should complain of his man. "I can't eat this and I can't eat that." "This doesn't agree with me." "I have a weak stomach. My father had a weak stomach before me, and my grandfather." In talking to your cells remember they have no reasoning intelligence. They don't talk back to you except in the way of discomfort when they are too discouraged to do their work. They don't say to you, "It isn't so." They have intuitive, instinctive intelligence, but not reasoning intelligence. They take your word, and you speak the word!

I wish we could all take a vacation from negation. I wish for one day we could exalt everything in our bodies. I wish for one day we could glorify our flesh. Too long we have been taught that the body is a miserable thing which we have to carry round with us, rather than the temple of the living God, the only instrument through which God can speak and express. Remember we are told that we must glorify God in the flesh. "Yet in my flesh shall I see God." Do we see Him there? We could. We must make the flesh a thing of beauty; refine it so that it becomes the delicate instrument which God meant it to be. We cannot express without it. Therefore, let us perfect it, and we perfect it by transforming our mind— by changing our potential from negative to positive.

* * *

Nothing new in the foregoing? No, nothing new—only physical science is now putting her hand in the hand of religion, and psycho-somatic medicine is giving us the proof of the admonitions which the Bible has given us for so many centuries.

Psycho-somatic medicine is giving us the clue, and it is reorienting our whole idea of disease. The entire picture of physical ailments is changing before our eyes. No longer are we thinking that disease is something which comes from outside of the body, over which we have no control; something that through fate or the devil is wished upon us and we can do nothing about it. That is the old idea. Today we are coming to understand more and more that what happens to us comes from within; that it is what cometh out of the heart that matters, not something outside of us. It is what the heart says, what you really and truly believe and feel in the very deepest part of you, that determines your ill- or well-being.

When the word heart is used in the Bible it refers to the subconscious mind. They did not know the subconscious mind but they did know the heart. Norman Vincent Peale voices this idea, when he says, "What you believe in your heart—that is, deep in your subconscious mind—determines what you can or what you cannot do. So, if you practise believing that with the help of God you can overcome obstacles and achieve success, your will and imagination will flow forth together and, against that power, nothing negative, nothing in the nature of defeat, can stand. This astonishing power of positive thinking is the most marvellous secret of living."

The lie-detector of modern penology could be called the instrument of psycho-somatic medicine. The most hardened criminals, the most expert liars, cannot sit before a lie-detector and tell a falsehood without registering a change in temperature, heart action and blood pressure. There is some involuntary reaction within the body mechanism which knows when the harmony which is truth is being perverted, and will register that disharmony in the instrument through bodily changes.

Another proof which science has given us recently that the emotions directly affect the body is the discovery of the drug ergotamine tartrate. Migraine headaches are those periodical affairs which are supposed to pass down from generation to generation. They are a sort of explosive affair in the body from bottled-up energy which has not its normal outlet, and which accumulates to the exploding point causing terrific congestion in the head. Epilepsy is somewhere in the same family—perhaps first cousin.

For many years science has had drugs or sedatives which relieve the pain of the body by dulling the sensation of the cerebro-spinal nerves. But these sedatives would never touch migraine headaches. They would give no relief whatever. The searched-for drug that would act on the sympathetic nerves, and not upon the cerebro-spinal nerves, was ergotamine tartrate. The psycho-somaticists tell us that the sympathetic nerves are the nerves of love and hate. Ergotamine tartrate dulls the sensation of these nerves and relieves the migraine headache, but the permanent eradication of the headaches lies in the education of the patient towards his emotional states. Jealous, possessive love, or strong sensations of irritation or dislike towards another, are the negative aspects of the emotions which must be understood and overcome, for stimulation of the sympathetic nerves through these negative emotions tends to pile up nervous energy which, if not channelled off, explodes at periodic intervals.

The bacteriologist and the sanitarian have practically freed the civilized world from the scourges of sweeping epidemics, but in spite of hygienic and sanitary measures men, women and children continue to suffer from all manner of physical disturbances. Therefore, we are forced to search further for the cause of these disturbances, and we are led to the inner life of man—to his thoughts and emotions. When we enter the field of the emotional life we are entering unexplored territory. Man has discovered all the land there is on the earth, he has climbed the mountains, he has crossed the rivers, gone everywhere, seen everything, and now he is entering into a new era of unfoldment in a field that has barely been touched. He is now being called upon to face his own destructive emotional conflicts against which the most skilful doctors cannot offer immunity through drugs, serums or anti-toxins.

Heretofore we have thought that indulgence in a spell of the blues or a fit of anger was our privilege. It is still our privilege, but now we realize that we are not hurting anyone but ourselves in that indulgence. Is it wise that we should disobey the laws that God has given us? If we do, we cannot expect to remain unscathed. It is not God who punishes us. It seems like it, but it isn't. We punish ourselves.

*   *   *

So rename your world! Go out and find a new pattern, and a new name. You have the power to rename your universe. There is a sentence in the Bible which says, "Out of the ground Jehovah God made the beasts of the field and the birds of the heavens, and he brought them to man to see what he would call them. Whatsoever man called every living creature, that was the name thereof." Find out if it is true that you make your world what you name it! The most glorious thing that God could give to man was free-will, developing through hundreds of years of evolutive progress to a point where man could conceive the universe and develop his moral nature to the point where he could be given dominion over all things.

We are entering into that time when men will have full dominion, and will be conscious of it. We may seem to be far from it, but in the higher reaches of spiritual consciousness we can already see what the kingdom of God really will be when His will is brought from heaven into earth. To be brought from heaven is to be brought from the inner consciousness into the outer expression on earth. When you bring everything in your life from that inner source of knowing, and let it flow out into expression, you will find heaven on earth; not only health in your body, and peace in your soul, but absolute harmony in all your life affairs, because it flows out into the outer world and the world takes on the conditions which are reflected from within. What you think and feel in secret shall be shouted from the house-tops!

Talk to your cells. Praise your body. Tell your cells you believe in them and have confidence in them, and in their ability to do their work. But some will say, "I can't lie to myself. I won't say my digestion is good when it isn't." No, we don't want you to tell a falsehood. It would not register

B

anyway. But you can take some part of your body which is good, and you can take some things which your organs do well and praise these. You may think that your stomach can't digest butter. Well, you can live without butter. Glorify your stomach because it digests fruits and vegetables. Because it digests those beautifully give it the assurance that it can digest butter—if it can get out from under the tyranny of your negative affirmation.

The following couplet appeared in a British medical journal:

> "Eat all kind nature can bestow,
> It will amalgamate down below,
> If the mind says so!
> But if you once begin to doubt
> Your gastric juice will find it out!"

Rather than disparage your body why not say to your cells, "I have faith in you. I believe that God gave you the power to do your work. I believe that with His help I can give you the assurance that you can, and I pledge myself to work with you."

The body is sensitive. It registers every thought and feeling. Be tender with it. Watch how many times you say something derogatory about some part of it. Perhaps you are annoyed when something prevents you from doing the thing you want to do, and you say, "Oh, that old foot, that old knee, that old something." You may be giving it constant negative suggestions. It will follow them as implicitly as it will follow positive ones.

Bless your body always. Speak no word of condemnation about it. Praise it, and bless it in every cell, calling upon every cell for its perfect response. Remember we are called upon to see God in this flesh; to behold truth in the inward parts, and to know that all our members are written in the book of life!

Our Uncharted Emotional Life

THE EMOTIONAL life of a man is as yet mostly uncharted country. There are few sign-posts to guide us. The sign-post of psycho-somatic medicine says that negative emotions cannot be indulged in for any length of time without some unwholesome effect upon the body. Our changing attitude towards disease is simply this, that instead of things happening to us from the outside we are beginning to realize that they happen to us from within. We, ourselves, are the cause of much of our discomfort and unhappiness; even of our accidents. For accidents, we find, occur when our emotions are disturbed, causing a slip in our muscular co-ordination so that we take a wrong step, or drop what we try to handle.

We used to take comfort in being just pleasantly incapacitated because it brought us sympathy and attention. People remembered us, and we received flowers and notes from our friends and relatives, if we were not ill too long. It wasn't an advantage to be ill over a number of months for your friends sometimes forgot you and your relatives stayed home. But there was something to be said about having a mild operation and a trip to the hospital. People like to talk about their experiences. But today when someone comes to see you and you begin to talk of your aches and pains, there is danger that you will be met with this new psycho-somatic look and be asked, "What have you been doing?"

Formerly we indulged in negative emotions willy-nilly. Our self-pity caused us to feel sorry for ourselves for weeks and months at a time. There have been those who have held resentments for years. A quick temper was often indulged in under the excuse that the father or grandfather had handed it down. Phrases like these are familiar to us all, "I can't help it, it is my nature," as though the quick temper had been handed down with the antiques. There seemed to this person no particular reason to be ashamed of the temper; at least not ashamed enough to try very actively to overcome it, unless the influence of a very wise or deeply religious person brought the knowledge that all these things are under our control. The deeply religious person has insight gained from the Bible which has always taught that these things are not of God, and we are not bound by any such inheritance. Jesus taught men not to accept any inheritance from an earthly father. The inheritance we should claim is the perfection of our heavenly Father.

The body is one of the most delicate instruments that can be imagined. It is more precise than the most perfect precision instrument. It responds to everything we tell it, and everything we do to it through the control of the subconscious mind. I like to call the subconscious mind the "straw boss" of the body. We give over most of the functions of the body to the subconscious. It would be terribly inconvenient in our busy lives if we had to stop and superintend the digestion of every morsel of food, its distribution through the body and its assimilation into the cells. We relegate all this to the subconscious. The beating of the heart, the circulation of the blood and the elimination of waste, are all taken care of with that perfect precision and order that is one of the marvels of life.

It is as marvellous as the order revealed in chemistry or physics. These laws of the universe are so exact there is never any deviation from them. When we first studied chemistry we learned about the periodic law. We knew when the derivatives of crude oil were first being tabulated that the sequence was so perfect that we could put down a formula in its proper place in the proportion of carbon and oxygen in relation to hydrogen, even though we did not know the particular substance which that formula represented. We could write the formula in its place, because we knew there could be no skipping over to leave a gap in that sequence, and we knew that sometime later we would find that particular substance, and it would correspond exactly to that formula.

So those of us who have studied physical science have come to have a profound faith in the underlying order of the universe and in the dependability of natural law.

The word nature is never used in the Bible in the sense in which we use it today. Nature has come to mean to us this dependability of natural law. In the Bible this power is referred to as God, not nature, but we know that nature is God. We know that God is nature, plus. The surgeon says, "I will take out this part which seems to offend, and suture the tissues together. Nature will do the rest." Or he says, "I will bring the ends of the bones together and co-apt them, and nature will do the healing." He tells you, "I will operate and the wound will heal in a few days." He does not say, "I will heal it," because he knows there is a power operating in your body which will do the healing. He is saying, "God will do the healing." The surgeon is a co-worker with God in preparing the way for healing. For is not an operation in itself a minor miracle?

* * *

The tension under which we live in these modern times produces muscular tension and strain with a great many people. Prolonged tension interferes with circulation, so the most common of all diseases are congestions of the blood ending in inflammation.

One looks over a long list of medical terms, each one ending in the same terminal—"itis". These present a formidable array of maladies to the average lay mind, yet they all have a common denominator. Each one is the result of the same process in the body. Appendicitis, arthritis, colitis, gastritis, neuritis, peritonitis, tonsilitis, are all familiar to us. The symptoms differ according to the tissue affected, but the cause is the same, and the changes which take place in the tissues are the same.

A parallel picture of congestion as it occurs in the body may be drawn from the picture of congested traffic on a city street. If the flow of traffic is blocked at any point the cars back up, one by one, until the street is congested, and nothing can move. If the congestion extends as far as the next intersection, the cross street also becomes congested; just so does one part of the body affect another part.

Nearly all negative emotions tend to result in tension. Tension causes fatigue, and overfatigue, in turn, results in tension, completing the vicious circle. By tension we mean tightening of the muscles and fibres. This constriction of the tissue shuts off the free flow of blood. Like the automobiles in the street, the blood cells begin to back up, and you soon have an engorgement of blood in that part. Continued for even a short time this results in inflammation. The cardinal signs are swelling, increased heat or fever, tenderness, throbbing and, eventually, pain, because of the increased pressure upon the nerve endings. Not only does the part become tender to touch, but it becomes painful to use or move.

Now let us go back. As soon as the cause of the bottleneck is removed in the traffic jam the automobiles begin to move, and the street is soon cleared. As soon as the emotional tension is relieved in the body the blood begins to flow again freely and all signs of congestion soon disappear. Anything that will relieve the tension will release the congestion.

The power of prayer acts as quickly and as directly as any material agency in acute congestion. This explains why acute inflammation responds more readily to spiritual therapy than the average chronic condition, for in chronic conditions the pattern has been impressed for a much longer time.

A friend, critically ill with pneumonia, was not completely convinced that he could be helped through prayer alone. He very much wanted the relief, but that it could come so simply seemed almost too good to be true, and he said, "It sounds so easy the way you tell it. If it is as easy as that why doesn't everyone do it?" I agreed that it sounded easy but perhaps it was not quite as easy as it sounded.

An illustration came to my mind—that of a strong man standing in a circle of his friends asking each one in turn to come and stand in front of him and fall backward into his arms assuring them that he would not let them fall. Simple?

Yes, and yet there probably would not be one who could do it the first time. He thought a moment before answering, and then, ill as he was, he turned with a grin and said, "Well, it would depend a whole lot on who does the catching, wouldn't it?" He had the answer in that brief question. It does depend on who does the catching, and it depends upon our absolute faith and trust in that "One" not to let us down. When we are sure that the everlasting arms are underneath, and that they will never fail to catch us, we can let go with the abandon of an expert swimmer who throws himself upon the water in perfect confidence that it will buoy him up.

When we returned an hour later his wife met us at the door with his sleeping-jacket in her hand. She said, "I want you to feel this." It was soaking wet with perspiration. "I have just changed him into dry clothes, and changed his bed, and he is sleeping like a baby." The fever was broken, the crisis was passed. Even though he did not profess a deep religious belief, that boy really knew who was doing the catching! He instinctively realized that there was a power great enough to take care of him. Believing this he relaxed all tension and the body did the rest.

We do not deny that germs enter the picture, but we are confident that the germs are accessories after the fact.

Something must happen in the body before the germs have an opportunity to do their work. Germs, like the poor, are always with us. Why do they affect us at one time and not another? Because the germs can begin their work only when the cell-resistance is lowered. Due to the congestion, the food supply as well as the oxygen for the cells is partially cut off, and this lowers the resistance of the cells so the germs find a favourable opening. Infection, then, is added to congestion. When the tension is released, and the congestion is broken up, the cells regain their normal resistance and the germs have no chance.

A doctor friend admitted all this might be true about an infection by pneumococci or streptococci, but he said, "Surely you would not say that would apply to the spirochete!—the germ that causes syphilis." "Why not?" I replied. "Surely you would not imply that I had more faith in the power of a spirochete than I have in the power of God!"

* * *

Today a different attitude towards disease and accidents is showing itself. Formerly the position of material science was expressed in that old phrase, "The fortuitous concurrence of invisible atoms." Today we are questioning the word "fortuitous".

We are coming into the knowledge that we are not helpless victims of invasion by outside forces, so much as victims of ignorance about ourselves. Our preoccupation up to this time has been with the universe outside ourselves. From now on we must know something more definite about the things inside ourselves. Must we take more years to arrive at the place where we say, "We cannot allow ourselves to be filled with anger, fear and resentment," because of the effect these negative motions have upon our lives? We are not children, but we have not yet learned fully what these emotions do, or how to master them.

You may say, "I have always had this miserable tendency to be irritated and vindictive. If someone makes me suffer, I want to get even and make them suffer. How am I going to overcome this?" You may think this is your nature, but it is not the nature God gave you. It is simply your belief about yourself. Fixed beliefs rule us more tyrannically than we like to admit. Some think that beliefs such as these were the demons which Jesus commanded to come out of the people and leave them forever. He commanded them to come out through the love of God.

That is why we have come to spiritual therapy as the answer to the need. Psycho-somatics can tell us what our emotions do to us, but psycho-somatics cannot help us to overcome those emotions. So we come back to religion to tell us how. Religion has always told us how. It has said to us, "If you have aught against your brother" don't go to the altar hoping that your prayer will get through. You must clear yourself first and free yourself of all hateful and vengeful feelings, then your channel will be clear, and when you raise your heart to God the Divine love will come through. Not before. You alone know what the truth is. You give the orders. Whether you know it or not, you give a report to your cells as truly as the captain of a submarine sends a report of his findings through the periscope to the men below.

Often in chronic conditions you may feel better for a few days and then be much worse. If there was something organically wrong would you not feel down all the time? Don't you see it is because the world looks brighter for one reason or another, and the cells take on new life for a few days? It is only after a habit has become so fixed that the cells no longer have the power to rise that we have those deplorable chronic conditions that are so difficult to lift. When we come to these conditions with prayer we must come conscious of a power far greater than any human power, for human power can seldom lift them. When we come to these functional or organic disorders where the cells have been paralysed and crippled with fear, we must bring a great hope. We must come with the "good spell", and the tidings of great joy.

What is that gospel and that great hope? It is that the life of God is all round us, surrounding us and filling us, waiting to pour into us if we can but open ourselves and free ourselves from these negative thoughts and feelings which bind us. Then we can "look out beyond the blue", seeing the icebergs, the mists and the fog disappearing, and know that all is right with the world. Then we never send a negative message down to the men in the submarine, and our body cells never have to labour under the negative influence, but can work and live happily and gloriously.

Dr. Alexis Carrel, years ago, proved that living protoplasm can live indefinitely if it is given perfect living conditions. He proved it by keeping chicken hearts alive. With the assistance of Charles Lindbergh, who invented a mechanical heart to supply the cells at all times with nutrition and oxygen, that protoplasm still lives. Doesn't that say something to us? Doesn't that rebuke us? You may say if that is the case, then you can live for ever. Who says we can't? I don't know that there would be an advantage in living indefinitely. I don't know that one would want to, but this I do know, that there is an advantage in always living beautifully, and completely, in wholesome, healthy bodies.

There is an advantage in never being ill. We suffer only when we have something to learn. When we have disobeyed, we may have to suffer for a while until we have learned the lesson, then that which has made us come to God is taken away. We do not continue to suffer when we learn to listen and obey.

I don't say we are never ill or that we don't need a warning, but such warnings are invaluable if they turn us toward God in prayer, "Oh, Lord, what am I doing or not doing? Lead me. Show me." When we ask earnestly and courageously, with a willingness to do or give whatever is necessary so that the lesson may be learned, then we are released and healed. Jacob wrestled with the angel of the Lord in the darkness of ignorance seeking an answer. When the dawn came he was lifted into the clearer consciousness of knowing which brings light into our darkness. The angel loosed him and he was free.

*   *   *

"How do you know that it is right to pray for a person who is seriously ill?" "Do you know the span of this person's life?" "How do you know that it is not time for this one to go?"

These questions were asked of Ruth Robison, and she gave the most beautiful answer I have ever heard. To me it is the perfect answer. It was this, "I don't presume to know when the time will come for you or anyone to die, but this I do know, that you need not die sick. You can die well."

Her statement rings true to me, and it is my belief that that is what mankind is going to do in the next few hundred years if we are not too foolish to waste time indulging in negative emotions of fear, resentment and greed. If we are led by the eternal verities of our Master, then we will come into the next forward step which mankind must take, and in which we shall learn to control our emotions and thus govern our bodies so that illness, weakness and indispositions become more and more rare. Then the Master's picture of the kingdom of heaven will be with us in reality.

The mystics have always known this, but not all the saints, for the saints suffered at times because of their feeling that the suffering was necessary. I grant you that suffering often develops a beautiful character, but how much more beautiful might it be if expressed in a completely harmonized body?

The belief that we have a God who punishes, and sends these things upon His children; the belief that we have a God who would drive us out of the garden of Eden, the belief in a God who could create His opposite, is passing. We no longer believe in an anthropomorphic God moving us round like chessmen on a board. We think rather in terms of an infinite power of life and light and wisdom filling the universe. It is not easy to conceive an abstract power which is infinite, yet so close to us that it is "nearer than breathing, closer than hands and feet".

This is the great step that mankind is taking. This is the present transition. This is why we seem to be in a state of chaos and insecurity. It is because we are reaching out into a concept of abstract, infinite energy, yet trying to bring that abstract idea so close that we can still call God "Our Father".

Physical science has changed our thinking. We cannot think of God punishing us any more than we can conceive of electricity deliberately punishing anyone. If God is infinite goodness He is "too pure to behold iniquity". Jesus definitely taught that God is all good, all love, all wisdom, all light. What then causes calamities and troubles to come upon us? Our own ignorance of the law. Our ignorance of the law will not save us if we touch the exposed end of a live wire, so our ignorance will not save us from ejection from paradise. We put ourselves out of the garden of Eden. We eat of the forbidden fruit which we were not to touch. We personalize evil and give it power. The way lies open the moment we wish to return to the garden and eat only of the tree of life.

Whether we are material scientists or spiritual scientists, whether we are physicists or mystics, we base everything upon the stability and dependability of God's laws. We cannot break those laws. We disobey them. We must learn them, and we must learn to obey them. When we disobey them we suffer, and no power makes us suffer but ourselves. When we learn them and live by them we are free. That is the Truth that Jesus came to live for; the truth He demonstrated and died for.

Psycho-somatic Medicine

A WOMAN went into a drug store and asked for—a bottle of psycho-somatic medicine.

The term is misleading, for the psycho-somatic approach to the solution of bodily ills belongs to, and has come out of, the world of medicine, yet the solutions it brings are not taken out of a bottle!

Psycho-somatic is a new word on our horizon. It is a compound word, and refers to soul-body relationship. Psyche is taken from the old myth of the lovely Psyche who saw her reflection in the pool of still water. Soma means body; therefore psycho-somatic deals with the effect of the mind and emotions upon the physical body and its functions.

Several years ago Dr. Flanders Dunbar took a group of research workers to one of the large hospitals to interview those who were ill, with the idea of discovering some of the common emotional upheavals back of certain chronic diseases like high blood pressure, diabetes and arthritis. They interviewed many cases in an endeavour to find a common emotional factor which might have been the cause of these disturbances. They were searching for a common denominator in the emotional life of the individuals who were presenting the same physical changes, and they needed a large number of patients to make their findings significant.

As a check on the patients in the chronic wards they also needed a corresponding group of normal people, so they went to the accident ward, thinking, as one naturally would, that the people in the accident ward had met with outside forces over which they had no control, and therefore would be free from marked emotional conflicts. To their astonishment and surprise they found those in the accident ward gave evidence of great emotional upheavals. It seemed that accidents didn't just happen. There was an emotional cause for them, also. Today from the figures given to us we know that eighty-five per cent. of the accidents occur to fifteen per cent. of our people, and those fifteen per cent. are the people who have emotional upsets. When you are emotionally disturbed your muscles do not co-ordinate, and accidents result.

Frequent articles appear in magazines and newspapers telling us not to drive a car after a tilt with the cook or a quarrel with our in-laws. They caution us to wait until the emotional system has become stabilized. Do not act while you have any active feeling of irritation, resentment or anger. Restore harmony and balance first, then act.

In an eastern camp, a woman in her eighties, who was wonderfully active, wanted to climb the mountain with the others one morning. Some of the group objected, saying, "Oh, my, you must not think of going!" She replied, "I will not go as long as you have the thought of fear for me. When all of you can get together and see me going in perfect safety, enjoying it like the rest of you, then I will go." They were reproved. She went, and did rather a better job than some of the others. She knew that as long as they had fear for her it would be unwise for her to go.

* * *

Psycho-somatics is the last great advance in the medical field, and it is the bridge which is carrying us over into the field of non-medical healing. It is the recognition by the scientific world, and particularly by the medical world, that the cause of disease is not what we formerly thought it to be.

Not all are willing to accept it in all instances, of course. There are many reservations. Not all lay people will be willing at first to accept this new attitude towards disease. But let us not feel irritated because they do not come to that one hundred per cent. acceptance at once. We should work with them at the point where we find them, never condemning anything in which they still have faith.

We should be very careful not to destroy faith wherever we find it. We need, rather, to respect, favour and commend faith on any level, and then seek to lift it to another level. For instance, when people come to Merrybrook, our Vermont retreat, they ask us, "How long shall I take my insomnia medicine?" or "Shall I continue to take what the doctor gave me for my acid stomach?"

Our reply is similar to the classical answer which George Fox gave to William Penn. George Fox was the founder of the Society of Friends and William Penn became one of his followers. William Penn came of a long line of military ancestors, and he was very proud of his sword. Yet he was very much moved by George Fox, and knew that Fox took literally the teaching of Jesus, "He who takes the sword shall perish by the sword," and it troubled him. So one day after he had joined the group he asked, "How long shall I wear my sword?" and George Fox answered, "Wear it as long as thou canst."

That is our answer to those who ask how long to take the drug or the pill, "Take it as long as you believe in it." Do not put it away saying to yourself that you are going to see if you can do without it, for then you will be defeated before you start. Your very question implies that you still have faith that it can help you, or that you may not get well without it. Rather than trying to do without it, try to know that there is a power to which you are turning which is greater than any material help. This is the power that is behind all the agencies, and which gives them their potency. When you turn to that power, believing, you will find that then you can do without the material help.

Dr. Carl Binger in *The Doctor's Job* speaks about "splinters in the soul". He says that more people are sick because they are unhappy than there are those who are unhappy because they are sick. Unfortunately the medical world cannot immunize us against our destructive emotional conflicts, yet we see more and more clearly that suffering and disease are not thrust upon us from the outside. They are not visitations of fate, chance of the evil one. They are not punishments except in the sense that we punish ourselves by our lack of knowledge and control, or our wilfulness and disobedience.

The cause is within us. The cure is within us. When we know this our concept of disease is no longer that of something fixed upon the body cells which must be purged, cut or burned away. It is not something coming in from the outside which we cannot prevent. Rather it is a change from within, and we must find the reason why the body changes its perfect pattern to vibrate to discord rather than to harmony. Psycho-somatic research is helping us find the clues. Incidentally, it is changing the whole attitude and approach of medicine toward the problem of sick bodies and confused minds.

But psycho-somatic findings do not offer the complete solution to the problem of controlling our emotions. We bring these findings to you because they are revealing. We are not offering you here anything that can approach the dynamic which religion and religious belief can give.

As we bring you these pictures of psycho-somatic findings, do not necessarily try to fit yourself into each one. Do not, above all, try to fit your friends into each picture! Get the picture, then remember it as you go out to work and pray for others. It might be wise if you let them make their discoveries for themselves.

Analysis by a friend of one's difficulties is not always the most welcome thing one could hear. Desiring them to understand a point it is sometimes better to find an article or a book which says what you wish them to know, and suggest they read it. This is Glenn Clark's "top shelf method". He always makes his students reach for challenging ideas. Discovering the truth for one's self not only saves face, but gives one the thrill of a personal achievement.

* * *

The medical profession has accepted the idea of emotional causes for the majority of stomach ulcers. Peptic ulcers have come to be known as the "wound stripe of civilization". The

Mayo Clinic states that out of fifteen thousand ulcer patients eighty per cent. were found not to have any actual physical cause for ulcer of the stomach. That means that eight out of ten were suffering from emotional disturbances, for in only two out of the ten could there be found conditions in the body which might have given rise to stomach ulcers.

The typical ulcer patient is usually between twenty and forty years of age, usually tall and slender rather than fat, as you might suppose, active, wiry, intelligent and ambitious. Patients of this type are aggressive and independent, keeping their emotions locked up and priding themselves on their self-control. But repressing all outer show of emotion is not conquering the emotion. You can't sit up on top of the boiling tea-kettle all the time! Most ulcer cases have had feeding problems as children, with histories of nursing difficulties and frequent colic as babies.

They are people who live in the belief of the inheritance of weak or sensitive stomachs from their mothers, or an acid stomach from their father's side, fully convinced they must have these weaknesses because of that family inheritance. Ulcer patients, especially men, are usually devoted to their mothers. The desire to escape from their own fear of being a clinging vine often makes them reach out for responsibility and gives them the appearance of being go-getters. Their ambition and activity may be only a cloak for this dependent pull.

One such ulcer patient is described as "high-driving and dynamic, and close to the mother". This man in particular did not get along well with his wife. Unless the wife repeats the pattern of the mother and to some extent replaces her, there may be a little friction. The patient described was sent to the occupational therapy ward to do wood-working. He was not satisfied with making a table as the others did. He made a table and four chairs, and ended by criticizing the instructor for the way he managed the shop! Aggressive, but with good intentions.

Dr. Harold Wolff of Cornell Medical School, was able to make some observations which are enlightening. He had a patient whose name was Tom, who was badly burned at the

age of nine by drinking scalding hot soup. This burned his
oesophagus so badly that the scars closed it up and he could
not swallow. A false opening was made into his stomach
through which food could be introduced after he had masti-
cated it, and Dr. Wolff was able to observe the effects of
the emotions upon the walls of the stomach. When Tom was
resentful, hostile or peeved the walls of the stomach became
gorged with blood. They became as fiery red as Tom's face
when he was angry. On the contrary, when he was anxious,
afraid or depressed the walls of the stomach became as white
as his face.

Emotional excitement will expand the arteries and more
blood is brought to the tissues. On the other hand, emotions
which tend to depress will contract the blood-vessels so that
less blood is brought to the tissues. We recognize these colour
changes in the face, but we have not known the corresponding
changes in the mucous linings of the body and the effect on
the functions of the organs involved. We have common
phrases which connect emotional reactions with the digestive
organs, like "I am sick of it", or "I just couldn't swallow it",
or "I couldn't stomach it". The sight of blood makes some
people faint, or sick at the stomach. With others a feeling of
embarrassment brings a rush of blood to the face. These
emotional results are visible and easily recognized, but Dr.
Wolff's observations depict the same results on the organs of
the body.

*　　　*　　　*

As we have pointed out, the cells of the body have intuitive
intelligence of a very high order, but they have no reasoning
intelligence. Therefore, when we excite them, causing more
blood to be brought to the part, they simply use the extra
blood to manufacture the particular secretion assigned to them.
An over-supply of blood to the stomach walls causes an over-
secretion of gastric juice, one element of which is hydrochloric acid. Let us liken it to a group of workers in a shoe
factory. When raw material is sent to them they make it
into shoes. They do not know how many shoes are needed.

They just continue to make shoes as long as you furnish them the raw material. In like manner, the cells of the stomach, receiving more blood through the stimulus of strong emotions, go on making more and more hydrochloric acid. The free acid in excess of the amount needed to digest the proteins irritates the lining of the stomach, and an ulcer is the result.

Someone has called the stomach "the sounding board of the emotions". The effect of continued anxiety and fear upon the digestion is damaging to a degree. In this case there is not enough blood brought to the walls of the stomach, so the gland cells cannot manufacture sufficient gastric juice to break up the protein food and it lies, undigested, in the stomach. The food ferments, and eventually a low-grade ulcer appears in the lining. Thus we see how two opposite situations can end in the same unpleasant results. Statisticians have reported that in England, during the time of the blitz, perforated stomach ulcers increased fifty per cent. due to extreme tension from anxiety and fear. A perforated ulcer is one that has gone through the stomach wall—a serious ending to either type of ulcer.

Dr. Walter Alvarez of the Mayo Clinic has gained a reputation with his treatment of stomach ulcer caused by over-secretion of hydrochloric acid. When he has a patient who has frequent emotional upheavals he tells them how to avoid an ulcer by using up the excess acid in the stomach. If they are upset at bedtime he suggests they get up at three in the morning and eat a hearty meal of protein—beefsteak, cottage cheese, nuts, etc.—to use the excess hydrochloric acid poured into their stomachs by their emotional orgy.

Is it not a travesty on the intelligence of a man that he should allow his anger to bring him to such a performance? Is it not time we should learn the subtle relationship between our emotions and our bodies? The price of not learning is costly!

Unfasten Your Emotions

ALLERGY is a word which has appeared on the horizon in recent years. In being allergic one is supposed to be sensitive to certain kinds of dust, pollen, or incompletely digested foods. But what is it that makes the skin or mucous membranes sensitive, and prevents the proper digestion of foods? One can go to Colorado to escape ragweed; sleep on kapok pillows to avoid inhaling the dust of feathers, sell one's pet parrot, and yet retain the sensitiveness.

Avoiding foods that seem to cause irritation does not permanently change the situation. They are but palliative measures. Where then can a cure be found? The first hint came to us from the study of children with allergy problems.

Dr. Hyman Miller and his assistant, Dorothy M. Baruch, made some experiments with allergic children. They found that those who were non-allergic expressed their feelings freely, telling their parents what they thought about them. The others, not being able to say what they felt, had asthma, hay fever, eczema, and various skin irritations. Dr. Miller says, "Like little cornered animals these children feared and hated the impact of their mother's rejection, as all children do, but they felt they could not bring their hostility into the open."

They were not like the little girl who was reproved by her mother and put in a wardrobe until she should be good again. The child was in there so long, and was so quiet, her mother was becoming alarmed, and opened the door.

"What were you doing?" she asked this precocious little miss of four. "Well," she answered, pertly and defiantly, "I spit on your new dress, and I spit on your new coat, and I was waiting for enough spit to spit on your new hat!"

Now, that child would never have the hives! She could say what she thought. But the allergic children, who cannot express their feelings because of some life experience, submerge their irritations, and they are out-pictured eventually in irritations of the skin or mucous linings.

A mother once told us how she helped her children and kept them from being seriously ill. If they showed the least sign of disharmony in their bodies in a slight fever or cold, or some stomach disorder, she would drop everything she was doing at the moment, call off any social engagement, and devote her entire time and attention to them. She did not necessarily put her hands on them, or even put them to bed; but she would stay with them and remain close beside them all day. She let them feel her love for them. She might give them things to play with in bed or on the floor, but her presence would be assuring them every moment of her loving concern.

She was giving them the sense of security that we give in the prayer group or the healing nucleus when we assure those in need of the constant and unfailing love of God. We are all little children grown tall. We need the sureness and constant feeling that there is a power that is great enough to answer everything and take care of everything, and that that power is right beside us always. This mother sought to give her children a feeling of her constant love, and they quickly responded by returning to normal.

* * *

Dr. Flanders Dunbar claims that there is such a thing as "emotional contagion". None of us who have worked in prisons or hospitals, especially in mental wards, can refute that.

"Emotional contagion" is the answer to the question which has been in many of your minds, "How about little children or tiny babies? How do they get these things? They can't think negative thoughts." Dr. Dunbar states, "The youngest infant can be infected with fear, anger or disgust, even more easily than with measles. The results," she adds, "appear in little homely ways long before they develop into major tragedies. But," she assures us, "by the same token the child can catch love and trust and respect."

Exposure of a child to violent emotions in the first year of its life, especially when that emotion is accompanied by violent action, can leave scars which endure for a lifetime. A child does not have to be in the room or actually hear the words of the quarrel, or see the action. It is in the very atmosphere, and they catch the vibrations. They are sensitive, some much more than others. Some grown people catch vibrations and can sense when they go into a room or into a home whether there is harmony, peace and love there, or whether there is disharmony, bickering and quarrelling.

My mother told me years before any of these things had been written what to do with babies who had severe colic. She told me babies have colic because there is contention in the home. "Take the baby away from the home and it will not have the colic," she said. "Take it back into the home surroundings and the colic will return. You may be able to take one person out of the home and it will relieve the situation, but you may not always know which one, so take the baby away!"

This brings us to Dr. H. S. Liddell and his experiment with sheep. He placed his sheep in a laboratory where they had every comfort. The only disturbing element was the sound of a metronome which ran constantly. We used to practise with a metronome when we took piano lessons, remember? Dr. Liddell set the metronome to fifty beats per minutes as the regular rhythm. At feeding time, however, he stepped it up to one hundred and twenty per minute. It was not long before the sheep learned that when they heard the faster beat it was feeding time. Without the smell of food, without the sound of anyone coming, or the rattle of pails or anything to tell them, they would go and lift the tops of their feed boxes ready to eat.

He left them in that rhythm until he felt they were perfectly established in it, then he increased the usual rate of fifty to eighty, and finally to a hundred. The poor sheep were greatly confused, for they could not distinguish between the hundred beats per minute and the hundred and twenty which was the key rhythm of feeding time, so they would go to the feed boxes and, finding nothing there, become so disturbed they fell rapidly into a "state of nerves" which, in humans, we would call nervous prostration. They had tachycardia, if one could apply such a beautiful word to the fast hearts of mere sheep. Their hearts were more irregular, also, and other bodily functions were upset. They finally refused to eat. They sulked, they bickered and they quarrelled with each other, and could not relax at night when lying down. They had insomnia. I wonder if they counted sheep!

When Dr. Liddell let them out to graze with other normal sheep they gradually recovered, but it took a year or more before some of them were normal, and even then recovery was contingent upon continued peace and rhythm in their lives. If they were brought back to the laboratory and to the sound of the metronome they would begin to tremble and suffer palpitation of the heart, as all the old worries evidently crowded back upon them. Some sheep did not even have to hear the sound of the metronome. Just the smell and atmosphere of the laboratory was enough to arouse all the old symptoms.

Commenting on this experiment Dr. Dunbar remarks, "If you think babies are tougher than sheep you are mistaken." That is why it is important to establish regular rhythm for a child.

Regularity and timing are very necessary. That is why it is important for you and for me, as children of God, to establish and maintain a rhythm in our lives. Each morning we need to keep our appointment with God to catch the undertone which will step us into the rhythm of the day. Then we will not be confused, bewildered, nervous, excited or uncertain, but serene, poised and sure. An army major read of Dr. Liddell's sheep experiments. When he realized that those sheep had the same neurotic symptoms from which he had suffered, he said, "I'll be confounded if I am going to be a sheep," and made good his statement by getting well in a few days.

We heard a story from a man some time ago which presents a perfect corollary to this experiment. He has had asthma for years. He told us that he had a partner in business, and they were very close friends, but the partner yielded to temptation and cheated him out of a good deal of money. It hurt him very much, and he found it very hard to forgive him. The hurt found its physical expression in asthma. He told us that he could not pray the Lord's prayer for a long time after this happened. He said to his wife, "I am not going to say the Lord's prayer again until I really forgive that man, because when I come to that part where it says, 'Forgive us our trespasses as we forgive those who have trespassed against us,' I just can't say it until I have completely forgiven him." Months went by: he finally thought he had forgiven him, so he was able to repeat the Lord's prayer again, but his body did not return to its normal rhythm, and the asthma continued. Here is the interesting thing. He forgave his partner with his conscious mind, but his subconscious did not forgive nor forget.

He told us he could go to New York or Washington, or any other city, where he visited art galleries, heard lectures, and walked wherever he wanted to go, without a sign of the asthma, but when he got off the train in his home town, often he could not get into his house without sitting down on the steps to take adrenalin so that he could breathe! The old memories and hurts crowded in from his subconscious mind as he came back into the familiar atmosphere, and brought back the response in his body which was asthma.

*   *   *

How then are we going to cleanse the subconscious and unfasten our emotions? That is the problem with most of us. How are we going to cleanse the lower strata of memories and erase the scars of old hurts, old inhibitions and frustrations so that we may be completely released?

An interesting observation in hypnosis brings out the fact that you cannot say to the subconscious mind of an individual,

"You don't want to smoke," "You can't drink," "You don't like the taste of alcohol," and get results, because it will not work the way you want it to work, and the reason is that the subconscious mind does not register a negative suggestion or command. It does not hear the "don't, can't or won't". It hears and obeys the words of action, "Drink, smoke; drink, smoke."

Instinctively many of you have learned that the denial method must be used carefully. Here you have the reason. The denial method has a place, but you cannot hope to lift a habit by repeating it to a person's subconscious, "You don't want to do this or that." Your statement is far more effective if it is positive. See how right Jesus was. Oh, if we would only follow Him! Always His words were positive. They were words of action, with never a don't or can't in them. But try to think of something positive you can say to a person with a sex perversion, a drug addiction, or an alcoholic habit that will cleanse the subconscious and free them of the desire.

We found it very difficult. Then we found a book by Dr. Cobb of Crowhurst, in the south of England, called *Christ Healing*. In it he gives a technique which we feel is sound—it is to infill the soul of the person to be helped with the Holy Spirit. He asks that Jesus fill that one with His love, and asks God to send the divine love into that soul in such volume that every appetite is satisfied, every need is met and every want is filled. He asks that he be filled so completely that there is no desire left.

Were these not the instructions of Jesus—that we do not fight anything, or try to overcome anything with force, but absorb everything negative in love? We tried this method of erasing the desire by the infilling of the Holy Spirit, and it makes us very happy to report definite results in many instances.

A fine couple came to us who wanted very much to go out and teach and work in the Master's service, but they knew the wife could not go on in the work they both so much wanted to do until she overcame her self-consciousness. She was very shy, inhibited and reticent, and this made her inarticulate. They felt it was psychological, but they did not know how to meet it. We prayed with them, and were very close to her, but she went home without anything having happened. She left us with the confidence that it would come through, for she was praying believing, and with true courage to meet whatever would be shown to her.

It was about three months later that she wrote us a beautiful letter in which she said, in effect, "My answer came to me in a dream. In the dream I looked into a mirror, and instead of my own face reflected there I saw a horrible mask. It was so ugly it made me shudder to look at it, and I knew it was a mask of jealousy."

How she knew it was jealousy I cannot tell you, and I doubt that she could explain to you, but to her it was a mask of jealousy. She went on to say, "As I looked at it I realized something I would not have admitted to you because I would not have admitted it to myself. When I was a little girl about three years old my baby sister was born. She was blue-eyed, curly-haired and precocious. She was dimply, soft and cuddly, so everyone looked at her, and no one ever looked at me. I was tall and stringy, with straight black hair and unprepossessing as she was fair and attractive, and I hated her with a hatred that was deep and black.

"As I grew up into my teens I found I had other things which would replace physical attractiveness, and as I became popular I lost my feeling toward the younger sister, but it was still down there, buried in my subconscious memory. It must have been, for that day I saw it. And as I realized all this, I saw the hand of Jesus come from the back of my head and gently remove the mask from my face. Then I saw my own face in the mirror, radiant, shining and lovely, and I knew I was healed and cleansed and released."

Health From Within

THE HUMAN body is made to respond to emotional stimuli and mental suggestion. If negative suggestions are continuously repeated and not channelled off in action, the normal responses are carried along for an abnormal length of time.

Disease is but the prolongation of emotional stimuli upon the body. The responses are perfectly normal, but they are not supposed to be carried over an extensive period. The abnormality is not in the reaction of the body, but in our understanding of the power of suggestion and emotions upon it.

Thus our attitude toward disease is gradually changing. Many now believe that whatever happens to us comes from within and is under our control when we understand what the emotions do to the physical mechanism. We are coming to believe that health comes from within, and that the cause of disease comes from within also. "By thy words thou shalt be condemned, and by thy words thou shalt be justified," rings in our ears.

If we were always at the mercy of fate, if the thoughts, words and deeds of others, or any set of circumstances, could control us beyond our power to prevent them, we would never be free. Yet Jesus said repeatedly, He came that we might be free. He came to give us the truth which would make us free. Was He not telling us that it is our own thoughts, words, and emotions that condemn us? He told us the truth when He said if we would abide in Him and let His words abide in us, we could ask whatsoever we would and it would be done unto us!

Fear is one of the oldest of the emotions brought over from our biological past, related directly to the law of self-preservation. In early times man could not live without a highly developed sense of fear, so that his bodily reactions would protect him, and protect him quickly. We are so constituted that when anything comes up before us as an immediate physical menace the body withholds every process except those which will get us out of danger quickly. The digestion stops when we are faced with immediate harm. It can wait. Assimilation and elimination are held in abeyance. Then when the immediate danger has passed, the body swings back to its normal function and these processes are resumed.

When the danger is imminent the body pours blood-sugar into the blood-stream, and the blood-pressure is raised so that the muscles can react with great agility and speed to get us under the fence or away from danger in double-quick time. I repeat, this is a perfectly normal and marvellous process.

As our civilization has developed and expanded it has eliminated many of the more immediate dangers which have confronted man. Today there are more subtle, more passive fears, and if these are not channelled off in action they become buried or submerged in the subconscious mind or memory. To some these are vague fears of death; to others the fear is that of loneliness, old age, or suffering; again it may be fear of want and insecurity. Today there are subtle fears of atomic war and the annihilation of mankind.

Whatever the fear, the body continues to react to the emotional stimulus in the only way it knows. The body has no reasoning intelligence. It has only instinctive intelligence, and it continues to respond to the buried sense of fear just as it would to the active, immediate, physical danger. We may be consciously unaware of any such fear, but the body is always aware, and continues to keep the blood-pressure raised beyond the normal needs of the body.

When the blood pressure is increased until it is pounding against the elastic walls of the arteries, the body finds it must protect itself. The instinctive recuperative intelligence of the cells says, "We must strengthen the walls of the arteries. We cannot let them break." As men putting up sandbags to strengthen the dyke against the rising water, so the body cells build in along the walls of the arteries, thickening them so they will not break through. The only place where this is not feasible is in the brain where the thickening would cause pressure against the brain tissue. Since the arteries in the brain are extremely thin, one of them may break, and the resultant clot of blood within the brain tissue causes paralysis. This is called cerebral haemorrhage, or a stroke. When in other parts of the body the arteries are thickened we use the term arteriosclerosis, or hardening. This has always been accepted as a disease, yet, in reality, it is a protective process against prolonged negative emotions, principally fear.

Dr. George Crile of Cleveland conducted many experiments on the effects of shock, which is acute fear. These experiments increased his knowledge of ex-ophthalmic goitre, or soft goitre, in which the throat is full, the heart is fast and the eyes protrude. He felt sure he could relieve these patients if he could operate and remove part of the thyroid gland. At last one of his patients who was very near death with this type of goitre gave him permission to operate, but while she was on the table and under the anaesthetic, the heart-beat increased so rapidly and the blood-pressure rose so alarmingly he did not dare proceed. She passed away almost immediately and Dr. Crile felt the cause of her death was shock due to acute fear. This is not the same type of fear that causes high blood-pressure, for that is a submerged and often unconscious fear.

Later, when another patient came to Dr. Crile he decided not to tell her he was going to operate and thus arouse fear. He said, "We would like to give you a new inhalation treatment. We think it is very effective. Would you be willing?" "Yes," she said, "I'm glad of anything that you may offer." So he gave her the inhalation treatment, which was ether, and he removed the goitre without the symptoms of shock which had come to the first patient, and she made a beautiful recovery. So for several years doctors from all over the country visited Dr. Crile to see him "steal a goitre", because he never again told the patient that he was going to operate. Dr. Crile learned what emotions do to people, and having seen human beings destroyed by ungovernable emotions, he constantly stressed the importance of their control.

* * *

It is not my intention to advise against operating, it is simply my conviction there may be better ways to handle the situation. The operative method is always there for those who cannot find a surer way.

As for the question, "Can we hope to overcome high blood-pressure?" the story of Beryl Sloop gives you the answer.

Mrs. Sloop had an ex-ophthalmic goitre and dangerously high blood-pressure. She had been unable to work and on a salt-free diet for months. She came to us one evening reeling like a drunken person, with blinding headache and her blood-pressure extremely high. The doctor had said to her that very day, "We have tried everything we know. There is only one thing we have to offer and that is a sympathectomy." She said, "What in the world is that?" and he replied, "That is an operation to sever the sympathetic nerves along the spine." "No," she said, "that's too much."

So she went on her knees and the Holy Spirit sent her to us. We talked and prayed together that night, and all that wonderful love that flows through Wally so unobstructedly equalized her circulation, relieved her fear, quieted her whole body and she was able to go home and to have a good night's sleep.

The next morning after a conference with her doctor she telephoned—"I am coming up there. You have an extra bedroom. My husband and I are going to live with you. I have just been to the doctor and he tells me that my blood-pressure is seventy points under what it has ever been. I want to know what it is that you have. I am coming up there to get it. We are bringing our bags and we are going to stay until I find it."

She stayed with us from January until late spring and she found the answer.

Always she had worked under high tension. She had undergone many shocks and carried subtle fears. She realized her symptoms were aggravated by the habit of losing her temper or allowing herself to become irritated. With us she received ministry in prayer and meditation daily and she learned to turn to God for help in relinquishing old habits. Gradually, under this regime, her goitre disappeared and her high blood-pressure became a thing of the past.

Dr. Alfred Price, Rector of St. Stephen's Episcopal Church in Philadelphia, holds that positive prayer will do more good than the prayer of denial. He feels that it is better to say, "God is taking away all anger, fear and irritation now," rather than say, "I will not lose my temper, I will not be irritated, I will not be afraid."

With Beryl Sloop the process of healing continued progressively over a period of three years. During that time she changed her entire attitude towards life. With Alice Newton there were two years of preparation and the healing came instantaneously and was complete. We accept the former more readily than we do the latter type of healing. When we speak of instantaneous healings, when we read Dr. Alexis Carrel's account of the man with a cancer on the back of his hand and wrist which was healed before his eyes as he stood there looking at it, we find it difficult to believe. Dr. Carrel said that so far as he could see the process was one of normal cicatrization speeded up like a speeded-up camera.

When we hear of a marvellous recovery like that of Dr. George Parkhurst's mother, Genevieve Parkhurst, who had a lump in her breast which the doctor wanted to remove, but who was completely healed through prayer, we feel it is almost incomprehensible. As she prayed alone one day a terrific pain, like an electric shock, went through the lump and down her arm. When she recovered sufficiently she put her hand where the lump had been, and there was a hollow place as large as a fist. The lump had disappeared. She graciously allowed me to examine her later and I could find nothing in the tissues or glands that did not seem perfectly normal.

*　　*　　*

These things seem almost impossible to believe, yet here are great physicists like de Broglie who has given us an insight into the sub-atomic world in the theory of wave mechanics, and who says that when we go below the atom into the world of the electron, the proton and the neutron, we are entering the world of energy. This is an unseen world, and the laws of that world do not coincide with the laws of matter.

This disturbs the physicists. Du Nuoy deplores this "gaping breach in the arrogant edifice of science". Could it be (and I offer this as a subject of contemplation) that the invisible world of energy back of the atom and upon which the atom depends, is the world of the spirit? Could it be that in our spiritual therapy we generate a flow of divine love and life through our being which touches this world of spiritual energy back of the atoms and causes them to arrange themselves in their original harmonious order, thus changing the molecules in the twinkling of an eye?

May it be that as we place our hand in the Great Hand, and open ourselves to the healing light, we touch with our other hand the invisible world behind the atom, and in some hitherto incomprehensible way bring these electrons, protons and neutrons into harmonious relationship with each other, thus immediately, without perceptible passage of time, establish normal relations between the cells of that particular tissue? It is not inconceivable.

Many things at which the materialist has scoffed are being made clearer every day in the light of the findings of physical science. The man or woman today who will not believe anything that cannot be registered by the senses is totally ignorant of the advance of physical science. "An electron is materially inconceivable, yet it is more perfectly known through its effects than a simple piece of wood," du Nuoy tells us. The invisible world is playing an important part in the life of man today, and physical science is moving up nearer and nearer to the truths which religion has always taught us.

This does not mean that science and religion will ever meet. They are opposite expressions. Religion must always be out in front of science. We lift our spiritual antennae into the unknown, and through our intuition catch fragments of truth not yet recognized by the rest of the world. Later, science moves up to check these findings, tabulate and classify them, and they become part of our accepted knowledge.

But modern science today draws closer to religion than it has for many centuries. Because it does, we dare to hope that the art of healing through prayer may again become part of the service of the church. It is our hope, as Friends, that perhaps some day healing will again take the prominent place in that service for mankind that it evidently held in the ministry and teaching of George Fox and the early Quakers.

It is not generally known that in addition to his famous Journal, George Fox left a book of notes which he called, *The Book of Miracles*. Fortunately, in 1932 Dr. Henry J. Cadbury discovered in London a catalogue of all the papers and books written by George Fox, and among them items in regard to this unknown *Book of Miracles*. The book itself was never published, and the manuscript was unfortunately lost, but the catalogue cites one hundred and fifty entries of cures attributed to Fox, and gives some brief information in regard to them which Dr. Cadbury has filled in from other records available. It is now published under the title of *George Fox's Book of Miracles*. Dr. Cadbury collected other references which showed that the reason this book was not brought forward with the Journal was due to the enmity of the times toward any thought of faith-healing.

Still "Man the Unknown"

EARLY researchers in psycho-somatics found something most interesting about diabetes. They discovered that deep grief uses up more energy than any other emotion.

In acute grief the body pours quantities of sugar into the blood-stream to furnish the energy needed. If the period of grief is not unduly prolonged the body will adjust itself, but if the grief is submerged and cherished over a long period the body continues to respond in the only way it knows by replenishing the system with more sugar.

The point made is that this is a perfectly normal reaction to an emotional stimulus. The abnormal side of the picture is a grief submerged and carried in the heart, or subconscious, so that the body continues to pour blood sugar into the bloodstream over months and years until the pancreas cells are exhausted. The pancreas cells make the insulin which causes sugar to burn up into energy, but with this excessive amount of sugar coming in all the time the pancreas cells simply cannot keep up with it, and they go on a "sit-down strike". They are too tired to try to keep up with the emotions, and stop making insulin. Then the blood-sugar is not burned up and runs free in the blood-stream, and we call it sugar diabetes.

The discovery of insulin by Dr. Banting was a wonderful thing. Introduced into the diabetic body it helps to burn up some sugar, but it does not remove the cause. In this sense it does not restore or heal; it relieves, and prolongs life. But lifting the submerged emotion, and cleansing the subconscious mind through prayer, has healed diabetes.

It is difficult, because diabetics often seem reluctant to discuss their real emotions. They have a tendency to deny any conflicts. Their first emotional conflicts are apt to be in submission to and resentment of parental authority. Sometimes they are even jealous of others in the family, but are ashamed to admit such jealousy. Insistent seeking through meditation and prayer will eventually conquer the stubborn ego and bring release and healing. To the diabetic we would say, "Do not live by bread alone. Live by the manna of the spirit." To those who have grieved too long we would say, "Focus your love on another and you cannot grieve, for love is joy." Jesus offered us His joy for the spirit of mourning. Live in that joy.

*   *   *

Arthritis is a very touchy subject and one which has long baffled medical authorities. Dr. James Halliday, the famous Scottish authority, says that most of the people with whom he has worked who have rheumatoid arthritis are restless, overly independent, high-driving people, and adds that many of them have a fussy, bossy nature.

Dr. Edwin Gildea of Washington University in St. Louis has studied personality factors common to individuals who suffer from similar ailments. He reported to the American Psycho-somatic Society that "patients with rheumatoid arthritis tend to be meticulously orderly". Most of us have prided ourselves on that and thought it a commendable virtue. Perhaps it is, but it certainly can hurt you when you get to be forty-five or fifty!

Dr. Edmund Weiss of Philadelphia has a good phrase which he applies to arthritis—"smouldering resentment". He explains, "The muscles serve as a means of defence and attack in the struggle for existence, and thus internal tension is most easily relieved by muscular action. When action is inhibited by repressions, the resulting muscle-tension feels like pain." Some of us can testify to that!

Under this smouldering resentment these high-driving people, with tremendous push, get into trouble. These are the kind of people who go after something and never give up. You will find men and women who have partners in the home or in business who are not as competent and efficient as they would like, and so they keep trying to bring them up to the standard they have set for them. Gently, it is true, with no outbursts of temper and without nagging, but persistently and consistently pushing toward a goal of perfection. They push themselves toward the same goal.

I know a woman who has not stopped for ten years trying to make her husband use proper English, and he is an Englishman and knows the most beautiful English, but does not always speak it. Why should this disturb his wife? But it has, and she has had arthritis in all the small joints of her body.

The perfect lubricant for the stiff joints is the oil of joy. The motto is nonchalance and relinquishment. This means that we must not try to think everything through and plan every small detail. Let us say, "Master, I am not going to distress my loved ones by working out what they should do and expecting them to do it. Help me to love my friends and those close to me and live with a joyous nonchalance, no longer trying to manage it all. Vouchsafe me sweet sleep when I lie down at night, not a restless tossing trying to work it out by my scale. Give me the grace to put the government upon your shoulders so I may be free."

We can learn to live without tension and strain. We can learn to live so that it doesn't make any difference whether things are upside-down, right-side-out or hind-side-before! This is what I should like to say to every arthritic, "Relinquish self. Relinquish too much pride in accomplishment for yourself or those whom you love."

A great lesson for all of us lies in a remark Jesus made to Peter. It was after the crucifixion, in the early morning when they were in the boats and a mist was on the land. As they neared the shore they dimly discerned a figure before the fire preparing breakfast and John exclaimed, "It is the Lord." They beached the boat, and found the Master had breakfast for them. After they ate they walked aside and the Master, turning to John, said, "Tarry here until I come."

Peter evidently asked a question, or was curious, and the Master reproved him. He said to him, "What is that to thee? Follow thou Me." That is our reproof, even as it was Peter's on that long-ago day. When we are tempted to be too concerned let us hear that question, "What is that to thee? Follow THOU Me."

* * *

M any phrases in common use may give us the key to the emotional causes of heart-trouble. When we say we have taken something "too much to heart", we are unconsciously admitting that we have allowed something to touch our emotional life deeply.

A fast heart, or an uneven heart action like palpitation are common results of disturbed emotions. Angina pectoris is neuralgia of the heart accompanied by a spasm of the chest muscles which causes intense pain. Clutching the chest with the hand is a characteristic gesture as the sense of stricture shuts off the breath. A recent film showed a jealous husband who had spasms of pain when he could not have the things he wanted just when he wanted them and in the way he wanted them. The picture was very vivid as he clutched frantically for his breath as though something was shutting off his life. Those who suffer in this way have very little realization that the cause of their suffering lies within themselves, and that all unknowingly they are shutting themselves off from life and love.

In other types of heart-trouble there is no pain; only a sense of great weakness as though the heart would stop and you had to stop with it. One of the surest ways we know to overcome heart conditions is to use that most beautiful of all gifts, and the most maligned—love. How, then, are we to help people cure their heart trouble? Love is the solution, as the English mystic Edward Carpenter seemed to know in the poem "As It Happened", included in his book *Toward Democracy*.

"Cross-legged in a low tailor's den . . . sick, sick at heart . . .
    he sits,
No God, No truth, No justice—and under it all, No love.

This is what is slowly killing him—no love. . . . O the deep,
   deep hunger of love!

The little heart once so strong, full-pulsed . . . stumbling
with strange uncertain motion, like one confused—now hurrying
on, now halting in its pace as near to stop. . . .

And the grave doctor comes and says the valves are weak,
and recommends rest and good food and fresh air, and other
things that are not to be had: but says nothing of that which
lies nearest to the patient.

So he drags through the days, ever more lethargic growing,
caring not much whether he die or live—thinking perhaps to
die on the whole were better!

When, as it happened—and this was the strangest of all—
quite suddenly, the most unexpected thing in the world, to a
casual little club which once a week he was in the habit of
attending, there came one night a new member, of athletic
strength and beauty . . . and the newcomer turning spoke
friendly to him, and soon seemed to understand. And from
that time forward came and companioned and nursed him, and
great waves of health and strength came to him, as to a man
who after the long Arctic night bathes in the warmth and
light of the re-arisen sun. . . .

   The body grows strong and hardy, and the little heart gathers
      and
   Knits itself together, and sings, sings, sings!
   Sings all day to its friend, whether present or absent."

Heart-disease is the leading occupational disease of business
executives. Dr. George Schwartz and his associate made a
study of heart disease in Wall Street. They found the frequency
of coronary thrombosis ran parallel with the ticker of the stock
exchange. "When the market went on a rampage," they said,
"hearts went on a rampage and out came the stretchers."

Justice Oliver Wendell Holmes once said, "A man begins a
pursuit as a means of keeping alive—he ends by following
it at the cost of his life." Dr. Connor of the American Heart
Association points out that these men become so tense they
can't relax. He observes, "They fight a game of golf—they
don't play it." Dr. Leo Bartemeier, associate professor of
psychology in Detroit, comments, "Even when they try to

play they work so hard at it no one has a good time—especially not they."

Even the insurance men have learned that the physical examination does not reveal the drive of hidden emotion which builds up the "high-tension load". Dr. H. L. Smith in the 1937 report to the American Medical Association said that coronary disease was "twice as common" among executives as it was among labouring men who worked hard with their muscles, slept like babes, ate anything and rose each day fresh and invigorated.

Another keen observation is that "The hard-driving money-grubber is psychologically like one who must prove her popularity by a lot of dance programmes and autographs." Or one who "wants more and bigger toys than any kid in the block".

When we say to people "Love can heal these conditions," they say to us, "How can we learn to love?" They actually ask us, and it is not such a strange question, either.

There was a period in my life when I felt that I was quite supremely happy and self-sufficient and rather looked down on people who seemed to be out-going and affectionate. This seemed to me to be rather poor taste, yet deep within me was a great desire for affection. Mine was the worst kind of snobbery—most of it intellectual. If people spoke incorrect English I almost denied them entrance into the kingdom of God! Now, when someone asks "How can I love?" "How can I start?" "How can I learn?" I understand, because I have travelled that stretch of road, and I know that they are not facetious but very serious.

* * *

But how *do* you? It seems to me we learn to love by being genuinely interested in others so that we listen to them with attention, actually hearing what they have to say. When you listen more than you talk, you are loving—that is, if you love to talk. When you talk more than you listen, when you don't like to talk, then you are loving!

When you are inverting yourself you are establishing the balance and rhythm that ensures evenness of the emotional life, and at the same time you are establishing the evenness of the heart and restoring its confidence. The love of other people helps the little heart to knit up its weak fibres and grow strong again, as did the heart of the tailor in the poem when he found real love and companionship.

Those who have only possessive love or jealous love, or who fail to find completion in merely human love, are often frustrated to the point of illness. These arrive at wholeness and healing only when they find the great divine love which is impersonal, which is never possessive, and asks for nothing in return. Much prayer, much quiet time, much giving of yourself is the surest remedy for release. Give not of substance or material things only, but give of yourself, of your interest, your concern and your prayers.

We are coming to believe that pride which is arrogant and rigid often reflects itself in stiffness in the physical body. We are coming to realize that hardness of heart, and lack of true feeling, may outpicture in the body in hardened tissue, even in the form of gall-stones and kidney-stones. At the same time it is believed that jealousy and envy tend to block the passages. There are times when a sense of blockage in one's life may refer itself to blockage within the body. For man is mysteriously and wonderfully made, and according to Dr. Alexis Carrell is still "Man, the Unknown".

Establish Your Identity

As you talk with your friends of many of these things you are going to meet with definite resistance. They are going to ask you, for instance, "What are you going to do with the facts of life?" "How can you hope to meet all these things with prayer?" "What are you going to do with the people all about you who are really suffering and are completely incapacitated?" "You say that evil is not an entity—that it is not the reality—but here are the cold, hard facts of life. What are you going to do about them?"

Glenn Clark meets these questions in his book, *The Soul's Sincere Desire*. The cold, hard facts of life which the materialist, the so-called realist, loves to bring before you, what are these? Dr. Clark says he has found them to be quarrelling, bickering and suffering, and he explains, "Fact comes from factum, to make or do. Are these facts of life identical with the realities of life? Not according to Jesus. To Him reality does not consist of that which is made, but of that which eternally is. Love is; quarrels are made. Joy is; unhappiness is made. Truth is; falsehoods are made. Life is; sickness is made." If you are forced to come down to facts, bring these before your friends.

In spirit every truth is already there. Furthermore, it is already in evidence if we could but recognize it, and claim it, as Jesus did. He will teach us His way and His secret if we but ask him. There is a power which we can learn to use as Jesus used it which will enable us to triumph over ills of body and of soul. To see reality, as He saw it, is to lift oneself into it. To see reality for another is to lift him into it. That is why we no longer beseech, beg and pray God to give us healing and substance and happiness. Why beg and beseech and pray for what our Heavenly Father has already given? He has given us every good and perfect thing!

For what, then, do we pray, and for what must we continue to pray? We pray for illumination. We pray that our consciousness may be lifted into that place from which Christ operated—the place in consciousness where we can see our good and act upon it; where we not only behold the land, but have the courage to enter in and possess it.

Elizabeth Searle Lamb has written, "Faith is made up of three elements: belief, imagination, and action. Belief in God, in his omnipotence, omniscience and omnipresence. This foundation for faith is the rock on which I build my life. This is the first factor. A daring imagination to dream out far enough to recognize the abundance of God, is the second factor. It is easy to dream too small a dream, to live too small a life. The third factor is action. By belief I throw back the screen that separates me from God's goodness; by imagination I widen my horizon until I approximate His pattern for me; then I step out now, today, and act!"

There are many reasons why we stop short of the third step and fail to act. The chief of these is a feeling of unworthiness. Many of us fail to establish our identity. An elderly friend came to Merrybrook one summer, and as he was leaving he was asked by another guest, "Well, are you going away healed?" Very humbly he replied, "No, I am very, very much better. I would give anything if I could have an instantaneous and complete healing. I believe it is possible for others. I know it can be, but I do not feel I am worthy." I would ask you, as we asked our friend that day, "Have you ever thought of changing your identity?"

Who are you? Are you a body with a spark of God in it, or are you a son of the living God inhabiting a physical body?

Are you a son of Adam, or the red earth, living under the laws of matter, or are you a child of the King living under the laws of the Kingdom? Is it not a matter of identity?

Had this man said, "I am God's child and I can leave here well because I know that He can and will heal me," do you think he would have gone home taking his infirmities with him?

Other men and women came to Merrybrook with much more desperate conditions and went home healed!

* * *

It is important that you establish your identity. Claim your birthright, and press your claim! Are we any less humble because we say we are children of the living God? Do we have true humility when we say "I am not good enough"?

God bless you, none of us are good enough in that sense. It is not a question of goodness. It is a question of identity. Just as going forth in the Master's service is not a question of being ready. If we waited to be ready there would be very few in His service. None of us are ready in the sense of being adequate. The question is only, "Are you WILLING?" If you are willing, He will make you adequate. There is no one in the world who is so humble as one who gives himself willingly, feeling deeply his inadequacy, yet trusting God to fit him to the task.

Many of my readers know Starr Daily and have read his books *Love Can Open Prison Doors* and *Release*.* Could any of you say that Starr Daily was good enough?

A blackened criminal, with his record on every prison roster in the country, he lay in solitary confinement very near to death when the Master, Himself, came to him, looked into his eyes, and changed his life by helping him change his identity. The more inadequate we feel and the more handicaps we must overcome, the more beautiful the fruit God will bring forth when His love turns us inside out.

To be inverted is to be converted. When our past is turned under and ploughed over it becomes fertile soil for God's growth. In his prayer of re-dedication Starr Daily acknowledges, "When I am willing to let Thee change my within, I shall have victory over my without."

Exalt perfection in yourself and in others! Give thanks for it; lift it up. Demand perfection in yourself and see only perfection in others. When we pray for others we do not ask

* *Published by Arthur James (Evesham)*

God for something for them, but we ask that the Holy Spirit may illumine them to that which already is. It is always right to pray for another when we pray to call forth the perfection in them. The innate will of every person is for perfection.

As we do this we learn that it is not a duty, but man's highest privilege to love his enemies, and to pray for those who persecute and despitefully use him. For in loving them we exalt the highest in ourselves, and at the same time help to free them from negative, harmful emotions. Love is the universal solvent. Pity is not the way to release. Pity accepts the condition. Compassion understands and absolves it.

The marvel of the human spirit is the ability to establish our identity with the highest. Years ago Evelyn Underhill phrased it in some of the most beautiful words that have ever been written. To think, she wrote, "That our small, derivative spirits, in humble willed communion with the very Source of our being and power, can grow and expand into tools of the divine love and redeeming power. . . . Only in that atmosphere (of prayer) can they expand from a narrow self-hood into personalities capable of being fully used by God on supernatural levels for supernatural work. That is holiness —the achievement of a creative personality capable of further-ing the divine action within life."

*   *   *

We travel from October to April from coast to coast, meeting with united prayer groups in the larger cities. One of the sig-nificant facts about these groups is their ability to rise above differences in theology. They are no longer interested in argu-ments about interpretation of the Scripture. They are seeking avidly, and with deep earnestness, to find the highest common denominator in our Christian and democratic tradition—the perfection manifested in the man, Jesus of Nazareth.

Not only are these groups interdenominational, they are inter-racial also, cutting across all lines of class division, imbued by the belief in the dignity of man, and motivated toward any sacrifice to bring about a society more keenly aware of the part it must play in the next great step of the evolutive process. Like men and women who have lived in a valley from which they have beheld glimpses of a very high place, they have climbed the mountain by many paths only to find that all the paths converge as they near the goal.

In his pamphlet, *Collaboration with Eternity,* Glenn Clark points out that space has been contracted until today we live in a "big park, which grows smaller every day". But he feels we are not yet ready to overcome time on a safe and sure basis. Only those who have persisted in climbing to the highest mountain peaks of prayer have gained a clear vision of what lies before.

Some day these small groups must multiply into the whole race of men. "The moral perfection latent in a small minority will blossom in the majority, as will the universal comprehension and love radiated by Christ. Sincere effort alone counts. . . . Those whose souls have been perfected in the course of their passage through their bodies, who have fully understood the conflict between the flesh and the spirit of which they have been the stage, have triumphed over matter, and they alone represent the evolution group who are the forerunners of the superior race which is to come." That quotation is not from a great theologian, as you might suppose. It is from the pen of a great physicist, Lecomte du Nuoy, in *Human Destiny.*

The great revolts throughout the world from Mexico to China have been in the agricultural field: far-reaching agrarian revolutions in an effort of people to get back to the land. This is highly significant. Not only is the effort to get back to the land, but to get back to the security and safety which nearness to the earth always signifies to men, for nearness to nature is nearness to creation and to God.

* * *

So we come to the next great step in the evolutionary process, only this step rises out of the physical into the psychological and spiritual realms.

The physical mechanism in man has reached the goal it sought to attain—the development of an individual who could think and remember, and thus could profit by the experience of all his ancestors. This evolution now goes forward by man's participation in it. Centuries are gained by eliminating space and time. No longer does the individual have to pass through thousands of years of adaptation. It is possible now to pool experiences and to learn from the errors of the generations which have gone before.

There rises slowly in the hearts of men a sense of the universality of the growing effort, free from purely personal advantage or narrow nationalism, to usher in the new race. No longer do men dwell primarily upon the sacrifices to be made. These are demanded and must be made, but they can be made willingly in the spirit of investment, rather than made grudgingly in the sense of loss or hardship.

By seeking to know ourselves better we are learning to know our fellow men. By seeking the unique inspiration of Jesus' teaching we are putting the stress upon the unity of our beliefs rather than upon the division of our creeds. Thus we draw nearer to each other, and nearer to God. We sense a new depth of meaning in the Master's statement, "My Father worketh hitherto, and I work!"

We realize that the future of mankind and the world depends upon our faith and our conviction that moral values are more important than any other. The highest moral law imposes a complete surrender of self in all its narrow sense. In this disinterestedness toward self we recognize the tremendous dynamic of Jesus' teaching. It represents an ideal which we recognize intuitively as a goal to be attained; an "incontestable ideal" from which we are separated because we have failed to establish our permanent identity as the sons and daughters of God, as co-workers with Him in bringing His will and His kingdom from the heaven of the higher consciousness into visibility upon the earth.

Rename Your World

WILL you consider with me the possibility of creating a new world out of scientific knowledge and accumulated faith? Have we not come to a place where it is necessary to rename and remake our world? Has mankind any longer a choice? Isn't it likely that unless we rebuild our world that it may be changed for us in a most disastrous way? Then the rebuilding will have to be done later and with rubble.

Perhaps we would do well to face some of these questions, and think on these things. Students of the New Testament tell us that this remaking and renaming of our world is part of the teachings of Jesus Christ. There are tremendous issues at stake, and it is our belief that the Master would arouse us from our inertia, and lift us from our indifference, calling us anew with the words He used of old—those words of power and positive, dynamic force.

We have not yet begun to live the things that He taught. We have not yet begun to scratch the surface of the things that He told us were true. We have not begun to believe the promises that He made. He said, "Greater things shall ye do if ye abide in me and my words abide in you." Yet we are afraid to step out on that. We are afraid even to mention it. We are afraid to say to people, "Believe and hear this dynamic message." Why are we afraid? Of what are we afraid? Afraid that we cannot live up to those promises or that belief? Afraid of ridicule? Afraid that someone will say, "It does not work"? Afraid they may say, "They prayed for this one and that one and it did not do any good"?

Is that what you fear? Why should we fear? Jesus prayed for the lepers and not all of them were healed permanently.

All were healed at the moment, but not all remained healed. Do we say that this was because His power was not great enough in each instance? Did He fail? Did God fail? Did God's love not come through to all of them alike? What then does fail? We, the children of God, fail.

We must learn to live these things that He taught if we are going to live at all. We shall have to learn how to talk because out of the mouth comes our fulfilment or our destruction. The tongue is a powerful organ. The heart which in the Old Testament was not called the subconscious mind because they did not know that word then, was the source of man's conscious action. Wasn't it the subconscious mind that was meant when they said, "Out of the heart the mouth speaketh"? "Keep thy heart with all diligence for out of it are the issues of life"? It is that which is in the subconscious, deep down in our belief, that comes forth and causes us to act as well as speak. "By thy words thou shall be condemned; by thy words thou shalt be justified."

It is only when we have trained and disciplined the heart, or subconscious, with positive thoughts and actions that our world will become positive and we can step up on top of the negative things that surround us and threaten us with destruction. Only then can we move out into that high place of knowing which belonged to Jesus Christ.

* * *

These are not easy things to teach. People are filled with prejudices—they have certain teachings against which they have formed a feeling of dislike. That is a pity because many of these things are part of our Christian tradition, and we should not have lost them. We have allowed ourselves to be influenced, and we have learned a language of frustration and negation.

I have a little phrase, "Take a vacation from negation." Try it for a day. See how many times you correct yourself when you make some claim that is not positive. If we are to abide in the words of Jesus Christ, and His words are to abide in us, then the words we speak must be positive words, for He spoke no negative words. His words were always words of action. "Go," "Behold," "See," "Stretch forth thine hand," "Arise," "Walk." Always they were dynamic words of power and action. They were never theoretical.

Never but once did He touch on anything that was not positive and it seems as though that incident was either not fully understood or not correctly reported. I allude to the parable of the fig-tree. Is it conceivable that the Master should have destroyed the fig-tree because it bore no fruit? Was our Lord not saying in essence to His disciples, "Look, I will show you that this law which we have been studying and which I have been demonstrating day after day will work in reverse. It will work for the negative as well as for the positive. I can curse this fig-tree and it will die. When we come back this way tonight it will be dead." And it was.

Yes, the law will work in reverse, just as an automobile will go backward as well as forward under the same power when the gears are reversed. That which you magnify tends to magnify or destroy you. We make our world what we name it. We make our life what we name it—though some do not yet know this. Jessie Rittenhouse puts it,

> "I bargained with life for a penny,
>   And life would pay me no more,
> No matter how I begged at evening
>   When I counted my scanty store. . . .
> I bargained with life for a penny,
>   Only to learn, dismayed,
> That any wage I had asked of life
>   Life would have paid."

We claim what we want and we get what we claim. When we hear this for the first time it offends us because it brings the burden of guilt directly upon ourselves. When men no longer have a personified power of evil to blame what will they do? If we take the devil out of the picture and do not have him there to carry our alibis we will have nothing behind which to hide. We have always hidden behind the idea that there is an evil power working against the power of good, and because of that other power it is impossible for us to be free to live always in the light of God's love. Because men have felt that they were subject in some degree to this second power it seemed impossible for them always to do the constructive thing. Hiding, they were not willing to face the issue.

Today we must return, or perhaps, come for the first time, to the belief in one power, and that power God, or good. There can be no other. We are told throughout the Bible that we should have no other God before Him, yet man instinctively brings evil forward and thinks of it in terms of equal power with good.

It is true there are inversions of good. It is true there are many things which seem to us to be directly the opposite of good. And they are. They are complete inversions of good, but they are still the same power operating. They are that power working in reverse. We are but seeing the negative aspect, as we see the negative and positive expressions of electricity. We know there are not two powers just because we see two expressions of it. We know if we cross the negative pole we will be hurt. The negative pole represents evil, the opposite of the positive pole, or good. As a rule we believe it is only when we touch or cross the negative pole, or evil, that we are hurt. But on reflection we know that if we cross the positive pole we will be hurt, also, even though the positive pole represents good.

I don't suppose there is anything which brings us such great suffering as a wilful disregard of divine guidance when we refuse to move with the current of divine wisdom and deliberately move against that current. We cross the positive pole and we suffer and it is not evil that has caused the suffering. We cannot break God's laws any more than we can break the law of gravity when we step out of a second-story window. We disobey God's laws, we don't break them. In disobeying them they break us. The things which befall us are the things which we, not understanding, bring upon ourselves. One of the things which we have least understood is the power of our words. We have bound ourselves by the chains of our own beliefs.

* * *

Think of the things that we say! Think of the beliefs under which we labour!

The common belief is that if you run into the path of a germ you are bound to have the infection which that germ produces. Perhaps we even go out of our way to meet it on its path, for we say, "We catch" a cold. I would not ask you to believe that germs are not real. They are more real to many people than God. We have made a god of science to the extent that we almost worship the laws of science, and believe in them more firmly than we believe in the laws of God.

The germs, like the poor, are always with us, but the germs are accessories after the fact. If the germ were the primary offender no one would escape. An epidemic would take everyone in his path and no one would be spared. But that is never true. Even in the Black Plague of the Middle Ages not everyone succumbed. There were always those who were immune. What gave them that immunity? It was not always those who were blessed with great physical vitality, for some of the strongest were taken. It is not only an immunity of the body. Is it not perhaps an immunity of the body through the spirit? The immunity lies in the consciousness lifted beyond the laws of the material world. It is moving out of a lower dimension into a higher dimension in which the laws of the lower dimension no longer apply.

Physical science itself is bringing us the answer, and it is the same answer Jesus gave us. It is the answer which Jesus taught and lived. It lies in the discovery of the laws of wave mechanics; the laws of the sub-atomic world. In speaking of these in his book, *The Road to Reason*, Lecomte du Nuoy writes, "We must establish the continuity between the two universes (atomic and sub-atomic) that are still separated; the universe of the molecules . . . and the underlying universe of electrons, protons, and neutrons, indisputable base of the first, but subject to different laws."

The two worlds of which Jesus spoke, one visible and the other invisible, are subject to different laws. "Blessed are the ears," wrote Thomas à Kempis, "that hear the pulses of the divine whisper and give no heed to the many whisperings of the world."

Some of us are no longer disturbed by the idea of infection because we know there is a higher law of immunity than the lower one of infection. We do not deny the law, but we deny that we need to come under it. We are not dealing with negatives. We are dealing with positives, and therefore we have no fear. Having been a doctor of medicine and knowing the fixity of general conviction about the power of germs, it amazes me to see how rapidly the world is accepting new light on this subject. We do not repudiate the laws of hygiene. We obey them, but we call upon a higher law for our immunity from them.

To claim something for yourself that you do not want seems to be the height of human folly. If one wishes, for instance, to be strong, why neutralize that desire day after day by affirming weakness? I borrow this paragraph from the book of a friend,

"One girl in particular I remember—a lovely personality— yet one who chose to grow in instead of out. In the ever narrowing circle of her thought, she became as a record, over and over repeating almost automatically the same phrases— 'I can't,' 'Not strong enough,' 'Life is so difficult,' 'The Doctor says,' 'I never could,' 'Mother always told me,' 'I have done all I could.'

"It is distressing to watch anyone succumb to the dictates of the imprisoned ego. The constant repetition of destructive phrases leads to exaggeration, to a strengthening of trouble, and usually to greater difficulties. We may long to sweep away these impediments, but the sad thing is that another can seldom sweep them away or lift them out of a life with any enduring effect. The owner must cast them out herself as she awakens to the value of life with its possibilities of achievement."

Thomas à Kempis wrote, "Know that the love of self doth hurt thee more than anything else in the world. With it everywhere thou shalt bear a cross. If thou seekest thine own will and pleasure thou shalt never be quiet nor free from care, for in everything something shall be wanting."

What were the demons that Jesus always spoke about, and ordered to come out of people? Do you think they were disembodied spirits that had come in and possessed them? Whether disembodied spirits or obsessions they were very real. When you correlate His attitude towards disease with His command to the demons you begin to have an inkling of what those demons might have been.

It is fascinating to study His attitude toward disease. When He went to Simon Peter's home and the wife's mother lay ill with fever, He rebuked the fever. He did not rebuke the woman. His attitude was something like this, "How dare you be here?" "How dare you come into this body?" "You are out of place. You do not belong here."

In this same way He commanded the demons to come out of them and never enter them again. Was it a demon of belief in a power which could hold a child of God in bondage that he rebuked? Was it this which he commanded to "come out"? Did He not say that He wanted to show us the truth that would make us free? He not only lived it, but He died for it. What was this truth? Was it not the truth of the existence of one illimitable power, greater than all others? This power was certainly the power of love, and He taught us that if we abide in that love, speaking the words of love, then everything about us would swing into the harmony and rhythm of life.

When you speak only words of accord, harmony and love then the power of divine love flows through you constantly, renewing you. As we give more and more of ourselves we become more deeply immersed in the universal life, and we are constantly renewed as was the milk in the pitcher which the herdswoman set before the gods of Olympus as they walked upon the earth. Each time they drank from the pitcher it was refilled. It is when we speak words of disharmony, discord, hate and resentment that the strength and vitality go out of us.

We need to watch and pray, and watch what we pray. We need to watch what we say even when we are not praying. Most of us have learned not to hate or be resentful. We have learned not to be angry or hold envy. But we have not yet learned to say positive words about ourselves and our world. We have not yet learned that it is unwise to claim things we do not want.

"But," you say, "I cannot lie to myself. If I have a pain I have a pain." That is true. But it is true, also, that you need not lie to yourself. You can tell the truth to yourself, and the truth is that as long as you claim the pain or the limitation of weakness it is not likely that any power can overcome it or help you to overcome it.

If you do not want the negative you must claim the positive. The positive is always stronger. When we fully understand the power of words we shall speak no more words of discord and disease, but speak only words of health and harmony. The law of harmony is the law of love, and the law of love is the law of God. The light will always overcome darkness. The darkness can never put out the light. Words create anew. Words of harmony bind together and unite in strength. Words of discord undo connections, disintegrate and tend to destroy. We must choose which we would use, the creative or the destructive law. We must choose this day whom we shall serve. We must choose this day which world we would create for ourselves, the one described in the first chapter of Genesis, or the one described in the second chapter.

> You own a garden so wondrously fair
> Even God's angels would envy you there!
> Its pastures are green, its waters are still,
> You lie down beside them and drink to your fill.
> Here are love and peace and abiding joy,
> With all of God's substance for you to employ.
> Where is this garden so wondrously fair?
> You say, "If it is mine, why am I not there?

I live in a world that is ugly and bare.
If I own such a garden why am I not there?"

*   *   *

What about the question, "Perhaps it is God's will for me
to suffer?"

If you believe it is God's will that you must suffer to be
disciplined, then that is true for you. But if you really believe
that it is the will of God for you to suffer what right have you
to go to the doctor constantly? Have you thought about this?
Do you want to seek help to cure you or ease the pain when
you think that it is God's will that you should suffer it? Are
you not seeking to disobey God's will if this is what you
believe?

There are people who believe they must be poor in order
to be saintly. Even such a remarkable woman as Muriel Lester
gave up a beautiful home to live in poverty in the East End
of London because she felt it was a necessary step for her.
Kagawa, similarly, thought it a spiritual necessity that he
live in the slums and share the lives of the wretchedly poor.
For the few these things may be necessary, but for the many
it is not necessarily true.

When we learn that in our Heavenly Father's house there
is an abundance of everything we no longer seek to clutch
our possessions and they no longer have the power to possess
us. Then we become stewards of things. They are no longer
our masters and we can use them freely. We take, receive and
give, and that is right, for in that way no one is bound, no one
is held, and we have no fear either of lack of money or the
burden of it.

Similarly disease has no power over us except the power
which we give it. Are you sure that disease comes to us
from God? God knows no iniquity. God knows no inharmony. God is love, kindness, tenderness, understanding and
compassion. Our Lord said, "If ye then being evil, know how
to give good gifts unto your children, how much more shall
your Father which is in heaven give good things to them that
ask Him?"

God is all life. How could live ever create anything less than itself? There is abundant life. This universe is full of life. The primordial stuff of the universe itself is life. What then shuts us off from life? Can it be our negative affirmations and beliefs? Many years ago Herbert Spencer knew that "man is ever in the presence of an infinite and eternal energy from which all things proceed".

In the middle of the garden of Eden God placed the tree of life from which man could eat all that he wished, but he was forbidden to eat of the tree of the knowledge of good and evil lest he die. And the serpent told he would not surely die. And he didn't. It only deprived him of the fullness of life.

Try always to say, "In the name of Jesus Christ and in the power of His love I can do anything." Paul said, "Of myself I can do nothing, but in Christ I can do all things." Was not Paul at times too busy building churches and establishing a great organization that he neglected to go back to the source of his power and touch again that Infinite life that would have kept him steady and in perfect health? When he was forced to stop and take to his bed, he would then come back in spirit to that which he knew and the Christ spirit would renew him. We are told that he would arise from his sick bed and continue his tasks to the amazement of all.

Tomorrow, if someone should ask, "How are you?" would you be willing to say, "I am strong in the Lord and in the power of His might?" And could you believe it? Most Christians are so pussyfooted it is quite pitiful. They wouldn't want to make such a statement.

Yet here we stand with the greatest power in the world and the greatest promises that could be given to man. Here we stand with a future before us filled with the things which eye hath not seen nor ear heard; things already prepared for them that love the Lord, and we hesitate because we think someone might think us queer. Try for one day to see only positive things. Try not to make one single claim that does not ring with the positive note of Jesus' own words, and others shall see in you a new radiance, and it will manifest in your body.

The early Christians had shining faces filled with wonder and glory. They dared not walk abroad in the day for fear of being picked out from the crowd and sent to the arena. Where has that glory gone? Why have we lost it? Who has taken it? Who has robbed us of our heritage? No one but ourselves. We are the thieves and the robbers. We are the guilty ones.

Oh, beloved, as never before let us pray in these days of the world's need for the courage and strength to speak words of command, backed by the love and authority of Jesus Christ. We have nothing of ourselves. For did He not say of Himself He could do nothing—that it was the Father who worked through Him? So in that name, and in that authority, and with the power of the Holy Spirit behind us, we should be able to say to men and women, "Arise and walk," "Stretch forth thy hand and be whole."

Did He not imply there was nothing gone, nothing destroyed, neither dead in that body? Remember the physical body will not tolerate anything in it which is dead, not even a splinter. The body will get it out. Anything you eat that doesn't belong must come out immediately. The body may, under extreme conditions, encase the foreign matter in a wall or sac so that it cannot be free in the blood-stream to cause trouble, but the living body will not allow anything dead to remain in it. So do not believe that you have dead nerves, dead cells or dead anything. They may be dormant but they are not dead. They may be only five per cent. awake, but they are alive, and because they are alive they can be more alive.

With the touch of the divine life moving through the cells they come into quickened life. Did He not give us authority to say to these dormant cells, as He said to Jairus' daughter, "Come alive," "Come awake," for they are not dead but sleeping?

When a crooked back straightens, when seemingly paralysed muscles suddenly take on new strength, either through prayer, the spoken word, or the healing hand, we see God's power manifesting. When we see a woman with a paralysed arm held tightly to her side suddenly able to lift it above her head we know the power of belief which had bound her was broken by the faith and conviction of those who were praying for her. These are not miracles in the sense of breaking a law; they are the operation of a higher law which has long awaited our recognition and use.

* * *

Paraphrase Coue's formula and repeat over and over, "Day by day in every way, in the power of the Lord, I am stronger and stronger."

Day by day you can rebuild your body. Every cell in your body except the sex and brain cells are replaced every year of your life. Why, then, are they always renewed in the same pattern? Because you do not change the pattern. Why not make a new frame of reference? Make a picture of what you desire and keep it before you, seeing nothing else, for we are "transformed by the renewing of our minds".

Annette Kellerman was told she was crippled for life and could never do what normal girls do because of a curved spine. She put a picture before her of Annette Kellerman doing all sorts of athletic and acrobatic stunts, and her body built itself into that picture until she became the world's champion swimmer with one of the most beautiful bodies the world has ever seen. Nothing can stand in the way of the human will backed by God's will when used for constructive purposes toward greater and greater life!

One stands before us with arms outstretched. He begs us, "Come unto Me and learn of Me." "I will teach you. I will show you all things." "Let My words abide in you." If we obey that call then our words must not be, "I am afraid," "I don't think I can," "I don't see how." Too many of us are like the man in Luke vi. 6. We sit with a shrivelled right arm forgetting that if we stretch it forth in the Master's work it will be made whole.

We are afraid to step out, not realizing that no matter how weak or shrivelled that arm may be, once it is stretched forth in His service His power will make it strong. None are ever ready for His ministry in the sense of being adequate. We would never go out if we waited until we were fully prepared. We are so full of imperfections we could not. But we are all made adequate when we go out in the name and nature of Jesus Christ. It does not take perfection. Jesus took Simon the unstable, Simon the mercurial, Simon the impulsive, and renamed him Peter, the Rock.

Let Him rename you! Let Him show you how to rename your condition! He can, and He will.

* * *

The things I have written here are embedded in my life and experience. Through them has come a knowledge and a certainty of tremendous healing power available to us today as in the days when Jesus of Nazareth walked the earth. I say them because of the things I have witnessed. They are the reason why I have written this chapter and this book.

Everyman's Search

THE BOOK of Job is the story of a man. Yet as one reads and rereads it one becomes alive to the fact that it is the story of every man and his search for God. Volumes have been written on the meaning of Job. The book has been called the "problem of pain", the "epic of suffering"; and everywhere scholars disagree over the deeper meaning of this—the great drama of the Bible. Mysticism in essence is the consciousness of oneness with God. The cry of Job is the elemental cry of the mystic in every man, "How can I find God?"

Through the ages man has sought to find and touch reality. The highest moral precepts are not enough. Creeds, doctrines, ritual and dogma answer for a time, but soon or late the human spirit breaks bonds with these, and seeks anew the person of the Godhead. Men want to be filled with the divine creativeness and power. They want to have some conscious experience of oneness with All-being so that their otherwise insignificant and humdrum lives may be lifted into meaningful union with all that is. This is an abiding need. Browning voiced it in immortal verse in his poem on Saul—" 'tis the weakness in strength that I cry for! My flesh that I seek in the Godhead."

The drama of Job begins with the lines, "There was a man in the land of Uz whose name was Job, and that man was perfect and upright, and one that feared God, and eschewed evil." That describes a man ethically sound and socially responsible—a good man. The plot of Satan in the drama is to prove whether such a man really knows God, or whether in adversity he will reject the idea of God and deny Him. Universally applied, this is the test of the human spirit in all lands and times.

Edward Howard Griggs used to say, "To be able to stand in the midst of darkness and live as though all about you was light is the final test of the human spirit."

Those who meet adversity with bitterness, and who feel there can be no God when tragedy and loss touch their lives; those who cry out for help and, failing to find it, sink into disbelief and despair, denying the very existence of God, these are the men and women whom Satan was picturing when he said to the Lord, "Put forth Thy hand now and touch all that he hath, and he will denounce Thee to Thy face!"

How often in these days do we meet the utter pessimism which Satan anticipated in Job, when men and women have lost all they held dear, and question that there can be a God at all or, if a God, that He can be a God of love and mercy and yet let such terrible things happen to His children! Their disillusionment is one of the most difficult moods to meet, and their black clouds of despair cast shadows over the entire world.

Disaster after disaster fell upon Job. The Sabeans took his oxen and slew his servants; the fire of God fell upon his sheep and destroyed them; the Chaldeans stole his camels; a great wind demolished his house, and killed his sons and daughters as they sat at meat. Through all this Job held fast to his integrity, so Satan said to the Lord, "Put forth Thy hand now and touch his flesh and he will renounce Thee to Thy face." So the famous boils appeared, covering him from the "sole of his foot unto his crown".

Even his wife could not comprehend a man who would not renounce God after such calamitous afflictions. Her advice was to renounce God and die. But Job reproved her as a foolish woman. "Shall we receive good at the hand of God and shall we not receive evil?" he asked. But his grief was great, and his bewilderment was even greater.

"Why? Why?" was his cry, as it is the cry of men generally when misfortune comes upon them. Job's cry echoes down the centuries, "Why should God do this to me? I have lived a good life." Over and over he protests, "I have not done those things which I was not to do. Why does God punish me?"

Then his theme changes, and he asks, "How am I to reach Him that I may argue my case with Him? How can a man be just with God, for there is no daysman betwixt us that He might lay His hand upon us both." Here is voiced the need to talk to God, and to have God talk to us. "Then call Thou and I will answer. Or let me speak and answer Thou me."

His friends could not answer the deeper questions of his heart. The courtly Eliphaz, the argumentative Bildad, and the blunt Zophar, with Elihu, the younger, more philosophical friend, all came and sat with him. They brought solace without comfort. One admires these friends of Job, however. In the first place, they came and sat with him upon the ground seven days and seven nights and none spoke a word to him! It seems incredible, but it is so recorded! They listened to all he had to say before they started to speak. That is superb friendship. When they did speak, they gave him the conventional answers, but these did not satisfy.

"Why is light given to a man whose way is hidden?" queries Job. How could they answer that? Job was asking one of the most profound questions man can ask of Most-high Wisdom. He was asking of God, "Why do you give us the light of knowledge and yet hide from us the complete reality?"

This search for God and reality is like a torment in men's souls. Job did not, at this point in his lamentations, see it as a blessed torment which never lets us rest until we find that for which we search.

That blessed torment to Francis Thompson was the "hound of heaven that pursued him down the days and down the years, and through the labyrinthine ways of his own mind". That torment is the uncertainty which inspired one to say to the man at the gate of the years, "Give me a light that I may find my way into the unknown." It is the torment which leads to faith; to that point where we can say with the rest of the poem, "Put your hand in the hand of God and that shall be to you better than a light and safer than a known way."

* * *

Job knew the majesty of God. In beautiful passage after beautiful passage he pays tribute to the power of the Almighty. "He removeth mountains, overturning them in His anger. He shaketh the earth out of her place; the pillars thereof tremble. He commands the sun."

Like David he asks, "When I consider Thy heavens and the works of Thy fingers, the moon and the stars which Thou hast ordained, what is man that Thou art mindful of him? And the son of man that Thou visitest him?" David put the question, How can Thou, being infinite, deal with finite man? Job in turn asks, How can I, so insignificant, deal with one so great?

An older Hebrew prophet declared, "Behold, the Lord's hand is not shortened that it cannot save; neither His ear heavy that it cannot hear, but your iniquities have separated between you and your God, and your sins have hid his face from you, that you will not hear." Job's sarcasm was biting when his friends enlarged upon this idea. "No doubt but ye are the people, and wisdom shall die with you! But I have understanding as well as you; I am not inferior to you. . . . I am as one that is a laughing-stock to his neighbour, a man that called upon God, and he answered him: the just, the perfect man is a laughing-stock."

The mistake of Job is the mistake of all men who know God intellectually only. Job's argument is, "I have lived a good life. I have obeyed the rules. I know there is a God. I acknowledge His mighty works. I have not sinned, and I will not accept the fact that my own sins are the cause of my distress." He thinks only of gross sins. That is his error. He has not committed this sin or that, but the subtle sins escape him, as they escape many of us. The most subtle sin of all, perhaps, is his own feeling of separation from God. He has not sought God through the heart. He has sought Him through the intellect and the reason, and He is not to be found.

Zophar speaks, "Canst thou by searching find out God? Canst thou find the Almighty unto perfection? It is high as heaven; what canst thou do? Deeper than Sheol; what canst thou know?" What can intellect do?

Many centuries later another great poet asked this question, "What can the intellect and reason do to help us in our search for God?" Dante, in the Paradisio, goes with Virgil through all the levels of purgatory where he is shown all the human desires and the struggle of men and women to satisfy them. He witnesses the torment of frustration and incompletion they undergo because they have not yet opened their hearts to the inflow of a higher wisdom and power.

As they come out on the plateau looking up at the mountain of transfiguration, Virgil, representing the intellect and the reasoning mind, bids him farewell. He says, in effect, "I can take you no further. I have shown you all I can. I cannot go with you into that rare, high place. I have taught you what I know. From here you must go alone." He leaves him with that beautiful benediction, "Thee o'er thyself I crown and mitre." That is, I make you your own emperor and your own pope, no longer under law, because loving the best thing best you have come to that place where you can travel alone.

It is then Dante looks upward and sees the beautiful face of Beatrice which to him represents all the goodness, all the purity and all the beauty there is. And he starts on that last upward climb alone; the ascent into the world of intuitive knowing where intellect and reason do not belong.

Job is slowly awakening to a higher consciousness, vaguely sensing the truth of God's immediacy, but not yet fully aware of it. "I go forward but He is not there," he continues in his soliloquy. "I go backward but I cannot perceive Him. I am conscious that He is at work, and I turn to the left but cannot behold Him. He is on the right hand; I know He is there, but He is in hiding, and I cannot see Him." An old Quaker gentleman reading this passage to his class felt the weakness in Job's searching when he said, "Job, you have gone forward and backward, and looked to left and to right. Why don't you try looking up?"

The exemplary life seems all that is necessary to so many, many people. To be a good man or a good woman seems all that is required, until a crisis comes with its test of our belief. The declaration of Job is the declaration of many, "Even now, behold, my witness is in heaven, and my record is on high." Then comes a flash of insight leading to his final illumination, "I know that my redeemer liveth, and that He shall stand up at the last upon the earth. And after my skin hath been thus destroyed, yet from my flesh shall I see God Whom I shall see for myself, and mine eyes shall behold, and not another."

There it is; there is the secret of his search and of all men's search—"Whom I shall see for myself, and mine eyes shall behold and not another." Not knowing God with the mind, but knowing Him in the heart! Not knowing Him through a mediator, but knowing Him of oneself.

* * *

A group of students in a theological college asked a very learned professor to read the Shepherd's Psalm. He read it with great feeling and beautiful emphasis. Then someone called for a retired minister to come up and repeat the same psalm. His sweet face shone with an inner light as he said the same words with great reverence and meaning. When he finished there was not a dry eye in the room. Afterward, one of the students asked the professor why that was. The professor was honest and humble in his reply. "Well," he said to the young man, "I have studied the Bible, and I know all about the Shepherd, but you see our friend KNOWS the Shepherd!"

Eliphaz had advised Job, "Acquaint now thyself with Him and be at peace!" but Job had only known God through hearsay. Eliphaz tries to sum up all the arguments, but his remarks are cut short as God speaks out of the whirlwind, "Who is this that darkeneth counsel?"

This rhythm is a path that will lead to the place of under- to the humility which he finally reached when he was able

D

to say, "Teach me, and I will hold my peace: And cause me to understand wherein I have erred!" This is the beginning of the death of the ego and the unfolding of the cosmic consciousness which knows that nothing matters except this— the finding of God. It knows, too, that the fault cannot be elsewhere than within itself.

Out of the whirlwind of mixed emotions and turbulent questioning came that Voice, "Gird up thy loins like a man for I will demand of thee and declare thou unto me." As God speaks, Job sees himself against the backdrop of omnipotence and cries, "Behold I am of small account." "I had heard of Thee by the hearing of the ear, but now mine eye seeth Thee."

As God reveals Himself before Job's astonished soul he cancels his lesser self. No longer angry, rebellious, or self-righteous in his suffering, he gladly relinquishes everything, knowing it to be of small moment. He lays all his treasures in the dust. He gives them all, and as he makes the complete relinquishment he can sing, "He knoweth the way that I take. When He hath tried me I shall come forth as gold."

When we can accept our sorrows and defeats, our disappointments and our afflictions, without rebellion, but in great thankfulness, then we "shall not go the way in vain. We shall have good of all our pain," even as Job.

"Let thy gold be cast in the furnace,
Thy red gold, precious and bright.
Do not fear the hungry fire
With its caverns of burning light!

And thy gold shall return more precious,
Free from every spot and stain,
For gold must be tried by fire,
As the heart must be tried by pain.

In the cruel fire of sorrow
Cast thy heart, do not faint or wail,
Let thy hand be firm and steady,
Do not let thy spirit quail.

But wait till the trial is over
And take thy heart again,
For as gold is tried by fire
So a heart must be tried by pain.

I shall know by the gleam and glitter
Of the golden chain you wear,
By your heart's calm strength in loving
Of the fire they have had to bear.

Beat on, true heart, forever!
Shine bright, strong, golden chain!
And bless the cleansing fire,
And the furnace of living pain."

Adelaide Proctor.

One Gave Thanks

In the seventeenth chapter of St. Luke we find the story of the ten lepers. They stood afar off as Jesus entered a certain village, and they lifted up their voices and cried out to the Master to have mercy upon them. He told them to go and show themselves to the priests, and as they went they were healed.

One of them—and he a Samaritan—turned back, and with a loud voice glorified God and fell on his face giving thanks. Jesus asked, "Were there not ten cleansed? But where are the nine? There are not found that returned to give glory to God save this stranger." And He said unto him, "Go thy way: thy faith hath made thee whole."

One gave thanks. All were healed, but only one returned. Did the one give thanks just for the healing of his body? Was it not for the baptism of awakening his spirit had received in that healing for which he gave thanks? For he knew that he had found a great and wonderful thing—even the source of life itself. He had found the kingdom of God within him. Not alone was he healed of his affliction, sore as that was, but he was healed of fear of any affliction or misfortune which might befall him in the future, for he had found a source of help which he knew would never fail him. That was, indeed, cause for thanks.

Nor did he need to go to any higher authority to establish the fact that he was healed. He knew. He had been born again, out of the world of the flesh into the world of the spirit. From thenceforth he would manifest in a material body but no longer under the law of matter; he was free!

There is a vivid lesson in this story for one who, with great earnestness, seeks healing of the body through spiritual therapy. There is no doubt that a single-minded faith on the part of one person can serve as the channel of relief and healing to another, but there is doubt that the healing will be permanent unless the one healed returns to give thanks in the sense that the tenth leper gave thanks.

One who comes for ministry through prayer, returning now and then to medical authorities for a check up, is trying to operate under the laws of two worlds. They may, and often do, receive definite benefits, but the permanent health is deeper than healing of the body. We would not deny relief, or temporary healing, to anyone, but we yearn to see the one who gives thanks for having found the door to life itself. That one remains healed and brings healing to others.

It is often confusing to those who come to Merrybrook, to accept a former doctor of medicine as a metaphysician. They sometimes admit that they come with a greater feeling of safety because they know a doctor is in charge, and experience a little disappointment or chagrin when they realize one cannot operate in both fields at the same time successfully. I would give of all my knowledge and skill, but I find it very awkward trying to jump the fence—being a physician one moment and a metaphysician the next.

In Robert Herrick's delightful story of the Master of the Inn, the Doctor tells any of his guests who wish the advice of a medical practitioner to go to Bert Williams down in the village.

"He still practises," he explains, "and he can give you what you need. He will help you more than I could for he still has faith in the stuff."

The one who approaches spiritual healing for the first time often finds it difficult to understand why it is not necessary to go into a detailed history of their case, explaining the symptoms, and relating the treatments and diagnoses given by various medical men and women whom they have visited. To them it seems incredible that they can be helped through any method which does not demand a full case history. They are trying to render unto God the things that are Caesar's.

Jesus ignored all the laws and rules of materia medica when He healed. He made no inquiry into the nature of the condition to be met. He sought no history. To Him one born blind was not different from the one who had had sight and lost it. An arm shrivelled from birth or an arm shrivelled from paralysis or injury were the same in that they both could be healed. In fact, Jesus never recognized the testimony of the physical senses. He rebuked the evidence of disorder, and claimed the immediate presence of God's perfect order, which is wholeness. It hinders rather than helps us in spiritual healing to be made aware of outward appearances. To dwell upon your own symptoms and weaknesses separates you from the kingdom of God within, wherein your hope of healing lies.

* * *

In the story of the evil spirit who returned and brought seven others with him, Jesus made it quite plain that the evil spirit and his more evil companions came in only if they found the house empty. It is only when the one cleansed fails to invite the Holy Spirit to come in and occupy the place of the unclean one that the negative brood can enter and make the condition of that person far worse than before. One who gives thanks utters a very special kind of prayer. Gratitude fervently expressed lifts the consciousness. One cannot be negative when one is giving heart-felt thanks, for thankfulness and gratitude are positive emotions.

The heart sings when we read the psalms. Great hymns of adoration and praise not only send thrills along our spines but they lift our spirits out of anxiety and worry into a place of security and peace. In praying for another we can easily pray amiss if we allow ourselves to dwell upon the handicaps of the one for whom we pray. A wife wished to pray for her husband that he might have more strength and endurance to meet his task. In her prayers she accentuated the husband's lack of strength; she visualized his utter weariness at the end of the day and his need of greater vitality.

Her deep desire for him was showing in her own body in

the form of tensions. When she changed her prayer to one of thankfulness for the splendid vitality and health her husband had enjoyed for years, she began to say over and over again, "How wonderful it is that he can do these things and accomplish so much of what he wants to do. Even though he comes home at night tired, how thankful I am that through the night God gives him refreshment to begin the new day."

One can always find something that has been given through the years for which to offer thanks. Complete that thankfulness with the prayer of affirmation, "I have been given so much all my life I know that the same power which has led me thus far will lead me to the end."

To pray the prayer of healing we must be able to visualize a change for which we can give thanks. We must be able to see the opposite of that which we deplore. Dwelling upon the negative will never change it to the positive. We must reconstruct the situation, and see all the factors in harmonious order the way we would like to see them. In that way we reverse the power and it will flow in the opposite direction.

Hearing news of disaster, loss, illness or suffering we are prone to say, "Oh, that is too bad!" "What a shame!" "Isn't it a pity?" If we pray with those emotions dominant in our minds we pray amiss.

An illustration of prayer in reverse is to be found in the story of a mother who sought healing for her son. In this instance both a negative and a positive request were answered at the same time! When the boy was ten years old a tonsilectomy was performed after which he was stricken with paralysis and left voiceless.

Joseph grew to be nineteen years old. The mother never abandoned her faith that God would answer her petition for her boy's healing. She was even willing that God should visit an affliction upon her body if that would make Joseph walk again. One day the mother fell and suffered a spinal injury, causing partial paralysis. Immediately Joseph began to gain the use of his limbs and soon was able to sit up and began to walk. He also recovered full use of his voice. This is an example of noble sacrifice born out of a great love, but one questions the necessity of bargaining with God.

Neurotics exemplify this law. Neurotics are people who use their imaginations in reverse. Blessed with unusual powers of imagination and visualization, they tend to use these powers in the negative. Ask them to write out for you the things they would like to do or be or have in life and invariably they will attach a sentence stating why they cannot hope to attain their desire.

There is always a reason. Like the Greeks, they have a word for it, and the word is negative! But when the neurotic individual is inverted—and that means converted—so that all his powers work in the positive, he becomes one of the most lovable, successful and radiant individuals in the world.

* * *

As continuous gratitude and giving thanks are necessary for the continuance of healing, so certain disciplines are required of those who would help others find healing.

The prophet Elisha did amazing things after the mantle of Elijah fell upon him with "double the power" of the older prophet. Yet we are shocked by the incident recorded in second Kings. As he went up from Bethel the children ran after him, mocking him, screaming, "Go up, thou bald head!" He turned on them and upbraided them in his anger. The account says two she-bears came out of the woods and destroyed forty-two children! That negative attitude seems utterly inconsistent with all the mighty works Elisha was doing. But suddenly the meaning becomes clear, and brings us a lesson we want to remember.

When one lives in the higher consciousness of the immediacy of God, the power of His spirit is ever ready to flow out in redeeming, healing streams to all whom we contact. By the same law, if we forget our discipline, and react from the lesser self as Elisha did at that moment, we reverse the current in that second of unforgiving criticism or condemnation.

When the power which redeems and heals is reversed its destructive action is as swift and sure as is the constructive action of love and healing.

So those of us who know the law, and are privileged to use it for good, have far more need of discipline than others. Paul saw the sorcery of Elymas as something black and perverted, and called him an enemy of righteousness, inflicting him with blindness. Lenitive, healing words of love might have lifted Elymas into an eagerness to experience the rapture of God through whose direct power he could have done far greater works than by his acts of legerdemain.

If we, therefore, would have life in the form of health, happiness and substance, and have it more abundantly, we must look, move and speak only in the direction of life. If we would help others find life we must speak no harsh or condemning words. If we would bring healing to others we must close our eyes and ears to all evidences of the lack of life. If we would dwell in the garden of Eden, and bring others to abide there with us, we must eat only of the tree of life which is in its midst.

We must recognize the need of keeping ourselves free from the sense of the physical incompleteness we are called upon to see and hear in the world and the need of lifting our consciousness into the place of understanding where we are aware of the perfection which is the true reality. For the spirit of love does not know its opposite. The current of life moves forward, never backward. Seeming disintegration is but the sign of transference of life from one vehicle to another. The vehicle changes; life goes on!

A true follower of Christ lives in two worlds, even as the Master declared He lived in two worlds. He must know both worlds, and the laws of both worlds, as Jesus knew them, but he functions only under the laws of the spirit. When talk of evil and criticism begins, or any recognition of a negative power is spoken, he closes the material ear, and rises on the wings of his faith out of reach into the clear, healing air of the spirit.

He learns to render unto Caesar the things of the world, and unto God the things of the spirit. He lives in the world of spiritual law, but he operates through a body of flesh in a world of material law. Thus he becomes, as Jesus instructed, "as wise as a serpent and as harmless as a dove".

A true disciple of Christ must needs live in two worlds, yet he need be subject only to the laws of the spirit.

Meditations

IN MEDITATION

Your solitude is a cathedral.
You are the priest,
You are the congregation,
You are the choir and the organ
You are the music.
You are the altar and
The white, burning candles
And their yellow light.
Your solitude is multitude;
A crowd of witnesses surrounds you,
The Lord of Hosts encompasses you.
Your solitude is multitude.
Your solitude is a cathedral.   Anon.

Meditations

*   *   *

The Path of Meditative Silence

Our first step in meditative silence is to forget completely the physical mechanism. The body must be at ease, relaxed, comfortable.

The second step is a little more difficult for most of us. It is the control, or perhaps a better word would be the supersedence, of the mental processes. We are working for a state of consciousness which is beyond reason and above mental activity, as we know it in the form of thought. We want to rise above the mental processes far enough so that thoughts do not intrude upon the silence which we seek.

Some writers, speakers and teachers talk of emptying the mind. They are saying the same thing that we are saying. They want to get above the area of mental processes. It is wise to disregard the thoughts that flit back and forth. It is strange, but just as surely as you want to meditate you will begin to think of all the things you should have done, that you wanted to do and did not do. Just at the moment when you want to be most quiet all these thought activities will intrude and disturb you.

It may be wise for you to have a pencil and paper by your side. As you grow silent and still if intruding thoughts come to you, jot them down so that you may attend to them later, then lay down your pencil with finality. Little by little, as you practise, you will find it easier to step out of these disturbing thoughts and go on to another level where they come and go without disturbing you.

It is necessary if possible that you have the same hour for meditation each day; necessary that you have the same place, the same chair and surroundings. In other words, it is well to try to establish a perfect rhythm.

* * *

The object of meditative prayer is to catch the underlying rhythm and tune in with the currents which move through the universe in perfect sequence and perfect order. When Jesus withdrew into the mountain or beside the sea to pray alone, He was simply releasing Himself to become still so that He could touch again the universal harmony which gave Him perfect poise, perfect equilibrium and a source of constant strength.

Your appointment is an appointment with God. Seek to keep that appointment against everything that the world may ask of you. You are really seeking the kingdom of heaven. If your search is sincere it must come before everything else. Sacrifices may have to be made, but it is rather simple, after the first few times, to discover what must be done to insure quiet.

Why do we meditate? Why is the practice of meditation valuable to one who seeks the fullness of religious life? In meditation we are re-forming, rebuilding and remaking. As we are reborn into the world of the spirit we find we have many habits which belong to the world of the material. To accomplish the things we wish to accomplish, and reach the place we wish to attain, it is necessary for us to build new habits and replace old ones until we establish ourselves firmly in the full consciousness of this reality which is behind the senses.

* * *

The seven steps of meditation, which came to us gradually, we have called the seven "A's" since each begins with an "A".

Having conquered the first preliminary steps toward achieving stillness, we then find that the state of meditation is somewhere half-way between waking and sleeping. The body and the mind sleep, but some other sense becomes awake.

Sometimes a sense of drowsiness intrudes and this can be overcome by a sense of awareness; an awareness of a Presence in the room, one whom you actually feel beside you. A sense of this Presence flows through you, and because you are increasingly aware of this Presence, you are awake. It is this awareness which awakens an inner sense within you.

These two are the first "A's"—AWAKE and AWARE. The adjective which modifies these "A's" is ACUTELY. Acutely awake, and acutely aware! No longer any danger of sleep when you have this acute awareness.

To approach this state of acute awareness, there must be an inner listening—not with strain or effort, but with an intentness which compels stillness—the feeling that you could not hear unless you were very still. To listen intently, without strain, is to find yourself acutely awake and acutely aware. This brings us into a state which could be called another state of consciousness, an awareness of something beyond the things to which we are accustomed.

We feel lifted into a rarefied atmosphere, and problems and disturbances seem to be left behind. We cannot carry these into this higher air and so suddenly we feel wonderfully free, released and alert to great new wonders, new possibilities, and this brings with it the concomitant feeling of tremendous aliveness. Everything in us becomes acutely ALERT and ALIVE! There is nothing dormant, in a fog, clouded or vague. Everything is open and expanding into a great aliveness. ACUTELY AWAKE, AWARE, ALERT AND ALIVE.

We become aware, now, not only of a Presence, but of a vibration which is the current of life flowing through us in steady, even, rhythmical streams; there is harmony and we sense something of the immensity of God.

It was this awareness which caused the Psalmist to sing the great Psalms of adoration. *It is not something apart, but something of which we are a part;* not something divided from us in space, but something included in us. We then begin to understand what the mystics mean when they tell us that the macrocosm is repeated in the microcosm of the little human soul. In some beautiful way this soul can expand and lift itself into some measure of a tremendous cosmic infinity, until we stand in awe before God.

We stand in awe before God, and then, presently, a feeling of great nearness comes; a feeling of comfort, of being loved and of deep security. We feel cherished and cared for, protected, guided, nurtured. Suddenly we become ATTUNED to the full harmony and we become AT-ONE with the Source of all life.

At-one-ment! To become at one with that Source, to be conscious even for a fraction of a moment of that union, means atonement—the wiping out of everything that has been, with complete forgiveness, complete cleansing and the union of the soul with its Maker. ATTUNED and AT-ONE!

* * *

This is perfect peace. It is utter tranquillity. One desires only to rest in this perfect peace, deep quiet and absolute love.

It is in this centre that we are healed. It is only as we touch this centre that we are able to help others find healing, because here we touch the centre of life and the centre of divine love itself.

We have come to that place where GOD IS.

"Be still and know that I am God."

Amen.

For Help in Using Your Sensitiveness

Master, we feel your presence. You are very real to us. Teach us. Speak through us. Lift us up. Tell us those things which we need to know that we may serve you better.

Give us the secret of transferring our sensitiveness from the little things of life to the great things. We want our sensitiveness but we want to extend a sense, a touch, a contact from the lesser self to that Christ self.

Help us to know how to lift our antennae into the great open reaches of spirit so that we may catch those lessons and those ideas which are waiting to come in. Your love is like a great transformer which can take the electric power and step it up instead of down. Take the little me in each one of us and lift it up into Your pattern. Touch the innermost part of each of us.

Take away all the refuse, all the old lumber, all the waste, take away all the ugly scaffolding upon which we have built and struggled so long, and leave us the perfect building.

Thank You, Father.

For One Who Has Regrets

We should have no regrets. We should never look back. The past is finished. There is nothing to be gained by going over it. Whatever it gave us in the experiences it brought us was something we had to know. Let us be thankful for it.

Never for a moment think, "I have lost those years. What can I hope to do now?" They were years of preparation; a germinating time. There is much we think we would change if we could live it over. Those things are deeply etched into the soul of you, and the soul will not forget. Just be assured when the time comes again, as it will come, and you reach a crisis where you must choose, the soul will know the path you should take.

Lessons are not lost. "We have not gone the way in vain. We have good of all our pain."

If we could only believe this! If we could but know it we would be thankful and grateful, stepping upon that past into whatever the future may hold. When we insist upon looking back we crystallize the power which would send us forward, and it turns one into a pillar of salt. We must look forward, unafraid, with our eyes ahead. We learn to take life open-armed, knowing that whatever experience it brings was needed experience.

* * *

Whenever we have to stand and wait it is for a purpose—a purpose we cannot see. We must learn to abide in patience, and to accept, not in resignation, but accept that which is needed to build the perfect pattern and to be grateful and thankful every moment as though it were a precious time of preparation.

The Spirit within teaches you what you can use for His work in creating beauty, in memorizing beautiful things, in imprinting His words indelibly upon your consciousness, filling the storehouse of your heart full of the treasures He may want you to use. Lie down to sleep each night with the rhythm of universal love in every part of your being, saying, "I will know. I will be shown. I will be told."

Live each day in conscious preparation, and the door *will* open, and your feet *will* be taken into the paths where they should go.

The Pool of Bethesda, a Cleansing Meditation

Let us visualize the pool of Bethesda. It is a pool of crystal clear water surrounded by a porch or a portico with flat shallow steps of stone leading into the water. Part of the portico is covered. The legend says that at intervals an Angel comes and troubles the waters. If one can go into the pool while the waters are still troubled and moving, he is healed.

Here along the portico are lined the crippled, the halt, the lame. Here is one man who can rise only upon his elbow. He carried down to the pool and carried back each day, and he comes day after day. He represents those who wish and seek but do not find.

However, on this day, a certain Figure walks among those who lie on the flat stones. His eyes search and find the eyes of the cripple who has never been able to get into the pool while the waters were still troubled because there was no one left to lift him. Something passes between these two. The cripple senses power, and he feels the compassion of those eyes. He holds up his arm. The Figure draws nearer to him, looks down upon him, and asks him a brief question, "Would'st thou be made whole?"

Search yourself with that question. Do you really want complete wholeness? At first the question sounds idiotic, but what the Stranger was really asking the cripple was, "Do you want to take the full responsibility for your wholeness? Are you willing to use the health, strength and vitality of a perfect body, a sane mind and a serene soul to help others and to help bring in the kingdom?" All of this was implied in the question. "Are you willing to be made whole?"

The cripple tells his story. We hear him say, "I have come so many times to the pool, and always after the waters are troubled so many run ahead of me that by the time I can drag myself down into the pool it is too late." But when Jesus said, "Would'st thou be made whole?" he seemed to sense that here was one who could see into the depths of him, and who knew what it was he had to answer.

Perhaps for the first time he faced that question squarely and answered it. He knew suddenly that he did not need to go into the pool. The Master said simply, "Be thou whole," and he knew it was so.

* * *

Now we are going into the pool for a little different reason. We are going into a pool of divine love; a pool of healing waters which flows forever from out the throne of God. Whosoever touches this stream of love, whosoever steps into the current of these healing waters, will find healing. The stream flows endlessly from out the heart of God, through the hearts of men, then flows back again to the heart of God. It is a never-ending stream.

This is the divine circulation.

We are going to step into the pool. First we must take off our shoes. This represents the sloughing off of the petty things which trouble us and bring us nearest to the earth and bind us most tightly to the lesser self. We take off our shoes because this is Holy ground.

We put our feet into the water and feel its soothing touch. We step still deeper; we go in up to our waist. In this step we acknowledge the cleansing of the sex part of our life. It now becomes the centre of creative activity, completely cleansed of the appetite of sex, and dedicated to the divine purpose for which it was made.

As we are bathing in these waters we realize that nothing in the body, none of its desires, its urges, its instincts, can control us again. From now on these organs are our servants, never our masters. Anything negative which has come into our lives through this part of our bodies is washed away, and not even the memory of it remains.

The water comes higher as we take another step forward. As the waters come above the waist we feel the overcoming of the appetites of the digestive tract. From now on these will never be our masters again, but will serve us faithfully to keep the temple of the living God beautiful, clean, sweet and radiant. All the waste that may have accrued because of the misuse of the appetite is washed away. We sense that these organs are so marvellously made and so beautifully conditioned that they can handle any foods which are put before us to sustain us. We lose all of our conscious fear about food. I have known of some of the most remarkable healings of colonic congestion from just this meditation alone, for this is a divine cleansing. If one gives himself to it he will feel all the organs of digestion, assimilation and elimination respond instantly. One is freed of old fears, and they will never come back. From henceforth you will eat your food, knowing that it has been blessed. You will have no thought about it after you have eaten it. God has made a beautiful body to do all that you wish it to do without giving a thought to it, and now we give it completely into the keeping of Him who made it.

Our next step into the waters brings us up to our shoulders and the waters cover our hearts and lungs. The heart symbolizes the emotional life. Immersion of this part of the body brings the cleansing of all the emotions. Here again, we sense that from now on our emotions are our obedient servants, never again our masters. This is a powerful means of conquering negative emotions. The Bible has always told us that it is not what goes into a man's mouth that defileth him, but that which comes out of his mouth. We can speak no negative words, we can carry no negative emotions in the heart, no matter how deeply buried, that will not be out-pictured in the physical body. The cleansing of the emotions is therefore a tremendous blessing.

As we feel the waters of life press upon our chest we feel the negative things pass out, giving us a great sense of freedom and release. The heart is glad, and the little cells sing to the joy of their release. The lungs symbolize the divine breath which is the link between God and man. They are expanding now as we take in great draughts of God's breath. This is the breath of life; the life which created us; the spirit which was breathed into us. Divine breath is a rarefied oxygen. Drink in great draughts of that breath. Let your lungs expand and your chest rise, and your body become light with the intake of God's breath, so you can take the next step and feel the waters about your throat and have no fear.

The throat is the centre of our sympathetic nature. When your emotions are moved and your sympathies aroused, your throat tends to become tight. Before we cry there is a con-striction of the throat. As we feel the gentle water rise up round our throats we feel it washing away all the negative emotions of self-pity, resentment and hurt feelings, until we are filled with the compassion of God. The difference between "sympathy" and "compassion" is a difference of positive and negative. "Sympathy" acknowledges conditions. "Compassion" understands the circumstances but never acknowledges them.

*   *   *

Now we are filled with God's compassion and His compassion absolves everything in us. It clears all the blockages in our channels through which divine love can flow. It is the opening of the arms as they reach out to all who are heavily laden and come for help. We no longer say we are sorry for you. We now say we understand you. We love you. We exalt the perfection in you! Arise, take up all your troubles and walk with us in Christ.

As you go out from this meditation, you will feel a cleansing such as you have never known before. You have opened yourselves to love, and have bathed in the great sea of divine love. You have been filled full with the divine power of the Holy Spirit. You will find peace and serenity.

Tonight you will have the most beautiful and restful kind of sleep, and awaken to one of the brightest mornings you have ever known.

Because All the Way Through He Has Stood Beside You by the Pool.

The Ark of the Covenant

God demands of us the past. He asks us to bring everything to the throne of His grace; not only to give of ourselves, but to give of our memories. The Master says to us, as He said to one long ago who would linger to bury his dead, "Follow Me". Let the dead past bury its dead.

We pass through great crises when the waves of emotion are like a turbulent sea. The flood of our feelings almost submerges us until, in our desperate need, we cry for help. Then the covenant is made with the Lord, and we are lifted out of the churning water into the ark, where we can ride the tide and come over to high ground. This is the lesson of the ark.

We must begin again.

The ark cannot carry the past—there is not room. All that can come over are creative ideas, and they come in pairs that they may be fruitful and multiply to replenish our new earth. So we leave the past, and bring with us only the lessons which it has etched into our consciousness. These we carry into the new life. All else is left behind.

We come to rest in a high place—a new state of consciousness. The dove of peace bears the green twig in its beak, assuring a new life. We begin overleaf; we write a fresh page. The old self is dead; the new self is born. In this new self we shall find green pastures and creative fields.

We thank God for all that we have been through. We give praise and thanksgiving for the lessons of the past. Then we lay the past aside. It is gone. Let it go, and a great peace and tranquillity of spirit will come over you, dispelling confusion as the waters of the emotional flood recede.

The ark stands, life is secure, and as you look out from the high place at the vision before you, you know that it will be good, and you say, "Thank You, Father. I do thank You." Amen.

For Healing of Old Hurts

When we have sought to help ourselves as thoroughly as we can, when we have dedicated ourselves as fully as we are able, but still retain the scars from the old hurts, then, Master, help us!

Deeply embedded in our subconscious selves the old hurts await Your touch, and the power of Your love to soften them. We need that touch, each one of us.

Strengthen us so we may step out of the pattern that is marred into the perfect pattern which lies eternally in our souls awaiting our recognition. These hurts, like the scratched places on the record, make discords as the cycle of life passes over them.

Master, we seek the great cleansing of Your spirit. We crave Your touch in the innermost parts of us, in the deepest memories, smoothing out and erasing all the scars and hurts which life has left. Melt us into full submission. Break down anything that stands between us and the full flow of Your love. If there is something we need to know, we ask that You help it to rise into our consciousness, that in our awareness of it it may be eliminated completely. Let us see it against the backdrop of the perfection which we feel and see in You.

Make it plain to us how the higher self, which is like Your divine self, must forgive the other human part of us. If we are to love others as we love ourselves, then we must learn to love the little self which so often needs to be forgiven for doing the things we do not want to do and saying the things we do not want to say.

The Christ self must exalt the lower, human self, forgive it, bless it, and lift it up, until it gives less and less offence to the higher, more divine self. Help us to understand this, so that we may know the complete harmony in all our being. Thank You, Father. Thank You, Jesus. Amen.

For Those Who Would
Undergird the Kingdom

It is not always the most apparent or the most spectacular things which serve best in bringing in the Kingdom. It is not always the contribution of those who are able to work in public, who speak, prophesy or heal, which is of most value.

There are thousands who serve by the very serenity of their being. There are those who can take the fitful winds of life and bear them with composure; those who can pass through the storms and stresses of human living with great selflessness;

those who can take the blows of circumstances without flinching, and be made finer by the testing of their spirit.

It is such as these, tireless in their desire to heal, who can lay the soothing hands on the fevered brows and quiet the warring elements in workshop and home. It is these who undergird the kingdom of God on earth. To them is given the great task of supporting, welding together and cementing the strands of love and healing that are constantly being sent out over the world.

Only those who have learned an inner stillness, and who walk closely with God, can be trusted to sit at the loom of life and watch the threads as they weave the eternal pattern: make us aware of the pattern as it unfolds before us, so that we may receive the flow of universal life through all our days.

Be content. Be happy. Be serene. Know, above all, that in being dependable in the crises of life you also serve.

Thank You, Jesus. Thank You, Father. Amen.

For Overcoming Reticence

I would let go of all reticence, diffidence and shyness and allow the power of love to fill me.

I want to open a door, a window. I want to pull the blinds back and then the sun will come streaming in, giving a radiance in the soul which will light the whole personality, lifting it, making it full of colour and music. Release the music—the celestial music that has been bottled up within you—so strengthening and renewing the cells of your body in every movement and in everything you say and feel. Swinging through you, let it find its way through difficulty and tragedy.

Salute the miracle of it, so the great power of the spirit can bring harmony out of inharmony, and the discords become great full chords as the mixed sounds separate themselves into tuneful melodies.

The Master can take all the jarring notes and blend them into the full chord.

The harmony will come to the inner perception first, and you will catch it with the inner hearing. Daily tune your inner ear so that it may hear.

As you do this day after day the cross-currents will come into parallel lines, and your life will become a succession of singing days. Master, help us to forget ourselves so that we may be open. Help us to lift our eyes and release our vision. Strip us of everything that stands between us and the glorious light. We want it to stream into and fill us until we glow with Thy fire divine.

Thank You, Father. Thank You, Jesus.

Judge Not From Appearances

Would you help a child in need—a friend in need? Then do not see them as the world sees them. See them as Jesus saw them and would see them today.

He did not see the outward manifestation. He looked through to the reality. He would have us follow His example.

That last night when He lived in the body upon earth He met with the beloved ones, and as He broke the bread and gave them of the wine, He said, "Eat and drink in remembrance of Me."

Surely He knew they could not forget Him? Of what remembrance then did He speak? Was He perhaps saying to them, as He says to us today, "Eat of My Body, drink of My blood that you may become like Me; that I may actually live in your flesh and in your blood so that you will react as I react, think as I think, and see as I see?"

Is this not the real communion, the daily, hourly communion, so that He becomes so literally incarnate in us that we no longer see what the world sees, but are able to look through and beyond the appearance into the reality which He saw?

He did not see the twisted body or the crippled legs of the beggar at the temple gate. He saw a beautiful figure, virile, strong, vital, leaping and running. He saw it with such clarity, such intentness, that He held the attention of everyone around Him until they saw it, too, and the reality came into visibility. He said we could do it through His love and by the authority and power of His spirit—yea, even greater things!

As you go out this day may you know throughout your whole being that you are completely changed; that something has happened within you; that a new life, a new vision, and a greater understanding has lifted you into a higher consciousness of Christ Jesus. You have "touched the hem of His garment, and His love has made you whole".

We thank You, Father, Amen.

For Protection Against the Hurts of Life

It is the little hurts of life that go so deep, and it is from these the Master can free us by His love. The little irritations and the little hurts! Protect us from these by covering us with the mantle of Your love.

Let it fall over us like a cone of light from our head to our feet. Cover us with the seamless garment—the full armour of the Lord. There is not a broken place in it through which you can be made vulnerable. Hold it close about you, and wear it always.

Under its perfect protection, as long as you abide in love nothing can reach you, nothing can touch you, nothing can harm you, nothing can hurt you!

So long as you abide in love, never being critical, never irritated, never resentful, you can never be hurt again, for nothing can pass through this cloak of divine protection without being transformed into love.

The beauty of the armour of God is that it transforms everything which touches it into love. If someone sends you harsh criticism, if one speaks false words about you, or deliberately tries to hurt you, these negative deeds are not even sent back to those who sent them, for there is no boomerang in love.

Love knows no retaliation. Through the divine chemistry all are lifted up, transmuted and transformed into love.

That is the mystery which man cannot comprehend, that love has this great power of translating everything which is not love into itself. That is why we can love those who despitefully use us and persecute us. That is why we can love those who ignorantly and thoughtlessly hurt us.

Everything hurtful that is sent to us but adds to the covering of love which protects us, and by and by there is something in love itself which will lift up those who would hurt us. For they do what they do out of a great longing and need for love. They are but turned inside out. They are but showing the rough side of the garment.

If we can receive all these things in perfect equanimity and forgiveness, without negative reaction, little by little they, too, will come under the spell of love and change through its power. For your forbearance and your patience, your understanding and compassion, are the tools which God uses to redeem His own.

How beautiful it is! How beautiful the feet upon the mountain of those who bring the tidings of great joy! How beautiful, Master, that You can teach us how to turn these pricks and arrows of outrageous fortune into the redeeming love that can lift those who crave love, and who suffer because they hurt needlessly.

Thank You, Father. Thank You, Jesus.

VENGEANCE IS MINE

"Vengeance is Mine,
    I will repay,
This the promise we have
    been given.
Ours only to bless,
    forgive, and pray

God's love may cleanse
that soul for heaven.

"Each time we bless
    Or voice a prayer
For one whose soul
    still gropes for light
We loose some bond,
    wipe out some debt
'Til wholly cleansed
    that soul sees God.

For the Dispelling of Fears

Why, why should you be afraid? Why should you shrink? Even the violet hidden under the leaves will push its way through to show its loveliness to the world. No matter what its surroundings it stays pure and clean. It is filled with life and vitality that flows out and flows in again, even as it should flow in you. It can never be bottled up nor hidden.

Life must be an outpouring and an outgiving, a receiving and a sharing as the great river of life flows out from the heart of God and flows into the heart of man, to return again to the heart of God.

Look up and see. Look out and behold. Behold the glory of the Lord. Stand and see your salvation. The prison bars drop away and the blinds are lifted until the brightness of God's love pours in.

Stretch your arms wide. Open them and receive life. Open them wide! Welcome everything that comes. Free yourself from everything that holds you back. Step forth and let the light of His love enfold you.

Your eyes will be unveiled and uncovered and you will be given a great spiritual perception. An inner sight becomes alive and the outer will come into perfect alignment with it.

To everyone you meet, to everyone who crosses your path, open your arms, your love, your heart, as though you would take the whole world into them.

Let all the love in you flow out; let all the cramped-up parts of you burst forth like a flower unfolding in the sun. His love will sustain you and hold you. His light will show you the way and bless you.

Just thank Your Father, as we thank Him now. Amen.

For Help in Tuning in to
the Rhythm of Life

We want to become so quiet that we may catch the underlying rhythm of life. We want to feel the pulsations which swing through the universe, the pulsations of life of which we are a part.

We want to tune in with these pulsations and to be so released, relaxed and free of self that we can be carried along by that undertow. It is like a heart-beat; like the tick of an old clock—tick, tock, tick, tock. Hear it saying, "Be still—and know—that I—am God." If we are still enough we will hear and feel that rhythm through the day.

Practise it at night when you go to sleep. Practise it when there are disagreeable noises which you wish to shut out. Catch some sound that has a steady beat, and repeat to its rhythm, "Be still—and know—that I—am God." You will find confusion leaving you and a sense of order replacing it.

Slowly, as you continue this over the days, you will come to the place of inward knowing and you can replace "Be still—and know—" with other phrases: "I will know;" "I will be told;" "I will be shown;" "The words which I am to speak will be put into my mouth;" "My feet will be taken into the paths where they should go;" "The door will be opened before me;" "My path will be made smooth and straight."

Because I am still, and know. "Be still and know that I am God."

This rhythm is a path that will lead to the place of understanding. Everything will be made plain. You will feel that deep eagerness and urge that pushes you forward. Release it, and relinquish it into this rhythm of God.

Be very still, and know that when the time comes, when you are ready and conditions are right, you will be told, you will know, you will be shown, and the door will open. In this there is no effort, no impatience. Rest in His love and discipline yourself into tranquillity of spirit.

You achieve co-ordination of body and clarity of mind together with tranquillity of spirit so that the great cosmic forces can work through you to accomplish that which you were sent here to do.

Thank You, Father.

For Help in Finding Your Place

We cannot all do the same work. Many and varied are the expressions necessary to complete the pattern. The oak tree does not spoil its beauty by wasting its energy in wishing that it might be maple or the elm. The violet does not trouble the loveliness of its little face by looking up at the great trees and wishing it could be something greater.

Each one in perfecting its own pattern, each one following its own instinctive plan, each one living true to that which is within itself—this is the lesson we need. Never longing to be something else, never trying to pattern after another, but living true to that which is within, knowing that every part is just as important as every other.

What one shows in strength and power another shows in humility and loveliness. We are not alike. But as we grow in the grace of God we grow more distinct, and this distinction is in itself of a unique beauty.

God has need of each one. Ask only to be shown the fulfilment of your own plan in the divine whole. Thank You, Jesus. Thank You, Father. Amen.

For One Who Has Sinned

We have all sinned, Master, grievously sinned. If we have not sinned in the outward act we have sinned in our hearts, and we want the full absolution of Your love this day. We want to lift the feeling of guilt that is in all of us.

We know how You understand for You would not have taken the publicans and sinners to Your side, nor taken the harlots to Your heart and lifted them up as You did, if You did not understand us.

We can almost hear You say, "Child of My Spirit, it is not what you have done, it is what you are willing to do that I recognize. I love you because the most hardened sinner among you is the one who is most able to feel deeply.

"It was that very intensity of feeling that caused you to go down so far; but, beloved, it is that very intensity of feeling that can take you just as far upward. That is why I need you—because you have the capacity for feeling deeply.

"Your great capacity for love, your great willingness to give of everything, your great loyalty, even though misdirected, are more precious to me than those who are lukewarm in their giving. Let me touch the soul of you and direct that capacity for feeling into My service, even as I touched the soul of Mary Magdalene. Your guilt, as truly as hers, can be turned into pure gold.

"I can take all of you and all of your past life and transform it. So, from henceforth, never feel that there is an indelible stain upon you which My love will not erase. Hold up your head, unashamed, because in the alchemy of My love I have wiped the pages clean.

"Never again have any feeling of unworthiness. No matter what you may have done or left undone, it belongs now to the past. It has been taken away, and shall not even come into mind any more."

It is wonderful, Father. We thank Thee. Amen.

For Those Who Are Heavily Laden

Do you often struggle to lift what seems a great weight? Stooping over, do you use all the strength of your arms and back, yet cannot seem to move it or lift it? Do you work until you are exhausted by the effort? Then lift your face, my child, and say, "O, Master, give me help. I must have help."

O, beloved, one touch of His hand will remove it all! Whoever you are, if you could just put your hand in His, let go and stop trying, stop struggling, but just kneel there and trust Him with the trust of a little child, then, suddenly, you will look around and the mass will be gone. The great burden will have disappeared. It is no longer there! I can hear you say, "Oh, why, why have I struggled so long?"

Spend no time in useless regret. Do not sit weeping for the days, the weeks, the years that have gone, but stand upright; walk forward, the light before you, shining ahead. If you will do this, one year of your life will be richer than your accumulated years. It is not a question of time in length of years; it is a question of volume and voltage; of the amount of power that you can let flow through you.

The years are never wasted. They are but delayed. Give thanks for all that you have learned in the lesson that has been taught, knowing that all those of us who have gone the rough path and have stumbled over the hard places can go back and help the others who are coming along the way.

We know the road because we have been over it. We can guide you round the boulders, take you over the rapids, past the dark woods and up to the foot of the mountain. Give thanks, great thanks in deep gratitude. Put your hand in the hand of God and let your desire become a fulfilment.

Thank You, Father.

For One Who Would Forget Self

We want the utter simplicity of a child; a simplicity that the world may say is almost stupid, so naïve, so without guile, so unaware of itself that it never hesitates, but goes in where angels might fear to tread.

It seeks no word of its own, only the words which are given. It makes no decisions. It follows wherever it is led. It takes no pride in accomplishment, is never puffed up.

It knows no distinctions of people. It knows all are the children of one Father. It asks only to bring glory to Him who guides and directs.

Is He not pleading with us that we forget ourselves more completely—that we become as approachable and as outgoing as children? We want the open-armed love which is unafraid, always seeking, moving out, never withdrawing within itself, or being conscious of itself.

Let the tenderness and sweetness which is in the core of your being flow out to the surface of your life; a childlike sweetness which, when it is added to the training and the discipline, the study and developed talent, make these things of greater beauty because it gives them overtones and undertones, softens the contours, and makes a deep appeal to the hearts of others.

Help us to be like You in this, Master, that all may feel the sweetness of Your love in us. We would become as little children in utter forgetfulness of self, that we may serve You and those who would find You.

Thank You, Jesus. Amen.

How Jesus Heals

Is it hard for you to believe? Think for a moment of how Jesus healed. He had no doctor, no hospital, no nurses, no drugs and made no diagnoses, yet in an instant, with a touch, a word, a look, He healed all that came and they went away whole.

He is not two thousand years removed from us. He is here today. He stands by our side. He walks with us as He walked with those by the Sea of Galilee. His loving eyes touch us. His searching glance looks us through and through. He asks of us only two questions, as He asked of the man at the pool of Bethesda.

"Wouldst thou be made whole?" is the first, and what He is saying is, "Are you willing to accept life in its fullness and take your place in the life around you?"

If He restores you to health and strength are you willing to return these to Him, augmented and magnified in the glory of His service? His second question was, "Believest thou that I am able to do this?" If you truly believe He can, then in this self-same hour it shall be done unto you.

Sometimes we say we believe, yet we lack the courage to take the third step and act upon our belief. We have only to go in and take that which has been prepared for us. There is no need to continue to ask and pray and beseech endlessly. Go out today with the absolute conviction that what you ask for, believing, is already done. It awaits only your recognition and acceptance.

Say, simply, "Thank You, Father, Thank You, Jesus, I know that it is so," then go in and possess the land.

For Help in Overcoming Self-consciousness

All those whom we know who are confused and have lost their way, or those who are lonely and who do not know how to find love, those who are hungry and starved for affection, let us give them food. Let us give them the manna of the Lord, which is love.

Let us draw in, almost as though it were breath, the great impersonal love of God, and breathe it out again to those who hunger and thirst for that love. Breathe it in; give it out. In order to receive love we must give love. To give love we must become unconscious of ourselves.

When we go into a room and we feel shy, embarrassed and self-conscious, let us look at some one person in that room intently for a moment, saying to ourselves, "Here is a human being like myself. I wonder what he is like. I wonder whether he is happy. I'm going to find out."

And you will find all your shyness and your diffidence suddenly gone, just because you have projected yourself toward another.

When we are with those whose lives touch ours from day to day, even the simplest of them—the butcher, the baker, the laundress or the cook—just make a gesture of love. You need not say anything. You need do nothing more than let them feel the touch of your hand upon them. If they draw away remember they are drawing away from Him and they are drawing away because they do not know what they reject. After a while if you touch them again they will not pull away.

We have to do so little and yet that is such a tremendous little to some of us who have never deliberately reached out to touch another life. But that is the most positive bridge through which the circuit of love can pass and be completed.

What we want to learn is how to break down the barriers of self which keep us too conscious of being separate. We want to come into the divine knowledge that we are all one, one with each other, and one with Jesus Christ and our Heavenly Father. For this was the commandment He left— that we love one another even as He loved us.

For Clearer Perception

You are like a mirror catching the light and breaking it up into prismatic colours of wondrous beauty. Your power lies in being able to reveal the beauty in other lives.

You see others, often, as though in a mirror. You become aware of the real person, as well as the reflection. The power of inner sight enables you to distinguish the real person from the reflection.

Or you see them as though hidden under a mask, and your clearer perception removes the mask, revealing them to you as God meant them to be.

Increase in us this power of inner perception, Master, that "we may see what Thou wouldst see, and do what Thou wouldst do".

Thank You, Jesus. Thank You, Father. Amen.

For Help in Being Yourself

Jesus said to Nathaniel, "Behold, here is one without guile." He was one of the transparent souls, like an incandescent light.

A little more courage, a little more confidence and you, too, may stand forth shining and radiant. There is nothing you have to do but just shine; just be your self, no matter how simple, how fragmentary that may seem to you.

If you focus all the love of your heart in your Master's service, you become a pin-point of light that can send its beams further than many a great searchlight which dissipates some radiance on the edges of its shining.

We are not asked to be like anyone else. God wants us to be all of ourselves—no two alike, because it is this diversity in unity which brings the greatest radiation of His love and power.

In the process of evolution there was a time when reproduction took place through a process of fission, one little life budding from another continuously. This unbroken continuity was immortality. Then somehow in the great need of life's progress that was changed and we see two individuals reproducing a third, then going back into the universal whole, and we might say that in that change we lost immortality.

How short-sighted we are; how little we see! For it was in that very diversity that the greater progress was made for the development of the moral life of men, lifting us closer to God. We don't want to be alike. We can't be alike. We do not want uniformity. Never look at another with a great desire that your expression should be like theirs. Just be yourself.

For Release of Tensions

Let there be no tension in your body. Relax and let yourself go, feeling that there is nothing to do and that there is no effort. You are not trying to learn or to understand; you are not trying to pray for anything. You are just resting, just letting go, just trying to feel, to sense the Pentecostal power which is ours to use.

Feel that power flowing through you, warming you as the sun warms you, with a great sense of well-being, of safety; of being cared for and cherished. Feel that you are significant, that God needs you. Feel it keenly, this great need of you. How can He express without you? How can His work be done, His kingdom built, His heaven placed upon earth unless He can work and live and speak and express through you and others like you? Expand everything in yourself. Feel yourself stretching and opening like a flower to the sun.

When you are really released, you won't be restless. You will just be still, and yet in that stillness you will be aware of an inner light and a tremendous movement going on all round you and through you. You will sense the pulsating life and the creative power which is being released, renewing every cell, every fibre and tissue; every organ being strengthened and vitalized.

You feel it from your head to your feet. Your hands feel the warmth of it down to the finger-tips, yet you are perfectly still and wide awake, and you will realize that you are alive

with an aliveness which means perfect harmony. Every part
of your body in perfect unity, perfect co-ordination.

Thank You, Father. Thank You, Jesus. Amen.

For Help in Releasing Laughter

I want you to open an inner door, the inner door of laughter.
I would have you release a quality which has been suppressed.
There is a lightness within you, a lightness that is a gift of
the spirit.

This gift of the spirit helps to touch everything lightly,
no matter how serious, no matter how tragic, no matter how
heavy it may seem; it is the light touch, the lightness of the
thistle down, a lightness that meets all things with true
insight, looking behind the appearance and seeing the reality.
It is the insight which has made the great humorists of the
world. They have looked at what men have made and
laughed; it was not the reality.

Deep in you is this quality. Let it come up. Let it bubble
and flow. The living water always underneath will never
fail you and will stand you in great stead wherever you go. It
will meet every problem. This is a precious gift, this lightness, this laughter of God.

We thank You for it, Father.

For One Who Has a Creative Urge

The great creative life urges and pushes until it can find an
instrument through which it can work. We must release
ourselves into that expression.

If we could just give ourselves and give every ability and
talent, He could use it so wonderfully, but our resistance is
like a heavy crust, and we become less and less sensitive to
the push and the urge. Yet there is an ache in us that cannot

be satisfied; a longing that is not answered. We grope like one who sees dimly.

Wait upon the Lord in quietness and confidence and let these great creative urges come through. In the security of His love move out, unafraid; not just sitting and dreaming, not just letting the mind make the pictures, but giving them outward expression. Do the things you have the urge to do. Go forth expectant and put the little urge into great action.

Let the power flow through you, and all the ache will turn to joy, and all the longing will be filled. Your heart will know a fullness that nothing else can bring it. Let us lose our life in Thee, knowing that we shall be used wisely and made complete.

Thank You, Father.

For One Who is Too Eager

The bud opens slowly. The tighter it is, and the more firmly compact, the more beautiful are the petals it unfolds. Rather than be impatient, ask in humility for the reason for delay. There is always a reason.

Pray constantly, "Master, show me what it is that You would have me do. What am I to learn? I am willing and ready. Show me." When the time is right the door will open, and it will be the right door, and you will not hesitate.

It takes many hours of waiting upon the Lord to be able to distinguish between the things we would like to say and those truths which He would speak through us. Sometimes we say, "I am so willing" but what we mean is, "I am so eager." Relinquish the eagerness, my child.

Be perfectly content, like the flower by the wayside awaiting its day. Enjoy the wonder, the glory, and the beauty of life and relinquish your eagerness. Energies are being gathered together and centralized in preparation for a greater wisdom to speak through you and a greater love to operate in you.

The more we live in the awareness of His presence the closer He comes, and the more intimate is our relationship with Him until we talk with Him and He talks with us. Our power of inner hearing becomes more and more acute as we learn to listen intently to His guiding voice.

One of the great laws of the spirit is that we must obey. We must learn to listen and we must learn to follow the guidance which is given as we listen. Remember Robert Browning's:

"Looking in and around me I ever renew,
    With that stoop of the soul which, in bending,
        upraises it too,
The submission of man's nothing-perfect to
        God's all-complete,
And by each new obeisance in spirit I climb
        to His feet."

For More Abundant Life

There are some souls that seem to be turned inward, caught in a web of bashfulness and fear.

They look out upon the world with hungering eyes like little children who sometimes sit and watch other children in their play but who take no part. Sad-eyed children, who would give anything if they could get in and be one with those who romp and laugh, but there is something which will not let them go.

There is something in many of us which holds us back for years from tasting the fullness of life's sweetness; many of us not really knowing, not really being conscious that we are not fully living until something touches that innermost part of us and brings it to life.

It is this that Jesus felt when He said that He wanted to give us life, and give it more abundantly. He wanted to release all souls to the fullness of life. He wanted to break chains and set the captives free.

Often it was His great love and tenderness alone that could do it. He looked into the eyes of Starr Daily and drew him inside out, as a magnet draws a piece of steel. He inverted him. All that had been drawn in was opened with a great opening. He collapsed time for him.

Through our love and concern we would see His love release those for whom we pray, bringing out the little girl or boy into the centre of the play, seeing them catch the ball, swinging into the rhythm of the game, lost to everything but the sheer happiness and joy in the movement of life. We know that Your love is great enough, Master, and we thank You as we expose these loved ones to its redeeming power.

Thank You, Father. Amen.

For One Who Believes
All Things Are Possible

When the father of the epileptic boy saw Jesus coming, after the disciples had failed to heal him, he said to the Master, "If it is possible for you to help us in our distress, please heal our boy." In His answer Jesus implied, "Why do you say possible? All things are possible to him who believes."

In that power of belief we realize there lies an element of out-picturing. We must believe that it is possible. If we believe that it is possible we out-picture what we ask for, and see that it is already done. We see ourselves acting in that finished pattern.

Even though the movement is impaired today, we see ourselves in that imagination, which is the most divine creation in man, as doing the things we want to do, and would do normally. We out-picture on the screen of our imagination that which we believe to be possible. We see ourselves acting it, living it; we hear ourselves saying it, and we feel ourselves doing it.

We need only remember that the power of its fulfilment

lies within the intensity of our desire. What we desire greatly, and what we out-picture ourselves as doing, saying or being, will come into visibility and action. Nothing can prevent it. If we believe that it is possible it will come forth.

The Master commands, "Go forth and be thou whole."

Come Unto Me and
I Will Give You Rest

We hear the Master's voice saying, "I would give you rest. I would lay My hands upon you and release all strain and loosen all the tension in you.

"I would take you in My arms like a babe, covering you with My love and protection until you have a feeling of absolute safety and security. I would infill you with My very being, so that you will know nothing can touch you, or harm you or hurt you. Nothing can ever reach you, because it cannot pass through My love, and My love is always surrounding you.

"Rest in the quiet of this assurance, with a great sense of well-being throughout your whole body, and a conviction that every inharmony will be brought into harmony; every discord changed into the full, sweet chord of health, abundant strength and vitality sufficient for your every need. Above all, a radiance and a sweetness like a perfume will touch everything you do, no matter how simple or humble it may be. No matter how menial the labour, it will be made beautiful in the light of My love.

"But do not strive. Be eager only to feel for a while that you are permeated with this new sense of life and peace. When the time is ready you will know. The door will open and you will be made adequate. Until then, abide, and know My love goes with you."

Thank You, Jesus. Thank You, Father. Amen.

For One With the Gift of Humour

There are many instruments upon which the Master can play. There are many different melodies He can bring out of them. One of these is humour, sparkling, scintillating, gentle humour, which can laugh away more troubles than we may be able to pray away.

How gracious is this gift which comes only to those who catch the melody of life, and who are able to see beyond appearances. In some sweet, persuasive way of their own they can laugh troubles away.

If you have lightness of heart, and a bubbling humour, never let them be weighed down. Sometimes others deplore this gift in you and would smother it, but it is given of God, so augment it and glorify it. When a great humorist is born, who has within him the deep love and compassion of God, he can show the world, without ridicule, how silly it is and how foolish.

And the world loves him for it for they know there is no sarcasm, no bitterness and no condemnation in his humour. He can laugh at the twisted, distorted thing which comes out of some human effort, and help us rise out of it because, for a split second, we can see it with him, and it lightens the load and eases the burden.

Deeply intuitive, Mark Twain and Will Rogers made fun of the world. Never sarcastic, never bitter, they made many things seem ridiculous and lifted the heaviness of men's hearts by the very lightness of their touch.

Such humour colours the horizon with rare and beautiful colours. Cherish it! Never let it be hidden. We are thankful for all who have it. May they use it under Your guidance and for Your glory!

Thank You, Father. Thank You, Jesus.

For One Who Seeks the Kingdom

We must come to the spiritual life in perfect honesty. There can be no pretence. If one starts on the path thinking to find only beauty, peace and loveliness, then coming to that place where they are made aware of the necessity for discipline, they may want to avoid that discipline. If that is true, then it were better that they make no further attempt.

Many come, drawn by the magnetism of the spirit, with a sort of wishful thinking, then when they find it is necessary to use control and to be stern they feel cheated.

But you cannot come into this straight and narrow way without learning the hard lessons. The love with which the healing of the body and the soul is consummated is not sentimental love. It is not possessive love. It is not a love which asks anything or seeks anything in return. It is a love which relinquishes everything.

It is the divine love, and to find it one must feel the steel of discipline, and one must be ready to deny oneself often. Most of all one must subdue the impulse of the ego to force itself into positions of prominence.

When Jesus said to the sons of Zebedee, "Would you be willing to follow?" when they wanted first place for which their mother's great ambition forced them to ask, He knew they little realized what it was they sought. This is no child's play, and one should be careful not to come until one is ready to subordinate self.

There are definite rules of the spiritual life and they must be obeyed. Master, give us strength and courage to meet the tests; give us power to have dominion over everything in our lesser self that our ego may die, and we may be able to pass through the crucifixion and go with You into our Father's house to serve there in its many mansions.

Thank You, Father. Thank You, Jesus.

For Helping Your Children

When you are working for your own children, whenever there seems to be disharmony, the simplest and surest way to be of use is to drop whatever you are doing, sit down by their chair or by their bed. You do not need to touch them. Just sit there and assure them of your love. Let them feel your abiding love.

They may be playing or may be sleeping or they may be lying in fever. Sit there and cherish them and love them. Let them feel your love and care for them. Aloud or silently (whichever seems best), tell them how wonderful they are, what a joy they are to you. Tell them of the things that you look forward to, the things they do that make you happy. Keep talking to them silently. Spend half a day if need be, or all day. They will improve rapidly.

We all need assurance. Children need it, and you and I are children and we need the assurance of God's love. We need to know that He cares, that He cherishes us, that He holds us closely; that He is interested in us, and watches us, watches over us. This is not figurative speech but it is real and it gives us that sense of comfort and well-being and security which all living things need if they are to grow.

This is true of plants, animals, children, men and women. We need the sun, and the light, and the water of His grace. Now this little child, whoever it is, has been blessed.

We thank You, Father.

For One Who Stands and Waits

He also serves who stands and waits. There always must be those who have learned patience and are willing to stand. It is not always those who go forward who are giving most. They have their reward, even as the Pharisee who prayed in public, but he who stands and waits is the pillar upon which the Kingdom rests; his patience is the foundation upon which all must be built.

It takes great spiritual strength to undergird the temple of God, like the massive girders of the bridge, unseen, unadorned, and unornamented, and yet the bridge would not stand without them. It was this quality of standing firm, this quality of the rock, which Jesus saw in Peter, upon which He knew He could build.

Let the ache of tedious waiting become a light in the heart. Let it shine, warming the whole being, shining because it has done its work well. Feel His shoulder coming up under yours, lifting the burden with you, until the sense of weight is gone, and only the buoyancy of His strength is there. Live in that strength and your frustration and weariness will change to thanksgiving and glory.

In His name. Thank You, Father.

Nuclear Therapy

(The Use of Intercessory Prayer)

Nuclear Therapy

The Use of Intercessory Prayer

The Oxford dictionary defines the word "nucleus" as a "central part or thing around which others are collected". This is our reason for coining the term "nuclear therapy".

A nucleus is the living heart of a cell. Nucleus also implies radiation, and we think of our prayer-work always as having radiant lines moving out from a centre. We never hold a meditative silence with a group that is not inclusive of others beyond the group or nucleus.

If a group closes itself, limiting itself to the immediate members and those closely connected with them, they limit the activity of the power of God. The power of God's healing love can flow through a consecrated group out into the world and touch many lives.

Is it not a stimulus to our prayer effort to know that whenever there is an earnest group, integrated in prayer, the power reaches through them, not only to those present in the immediate circle, or those for whom they are particularly praying, but the healing power flows beyond them and finds its entrance where souls are ready, waiting and open to receive it?

It is good to remember when you pray alone or in a group that out there in the world there may be someone who, in deep despair, is crying, "Lord God, or whatever power it is that is greater than I am, help me," and the wonderful love and healing force felt by you and by the group moves into the heart of that one, like water finding its level, bringing a sense of great peace.

That one will never know, and the group will never know, and that is as it should be, for we are using the power of

Divine Love which asks no reward, no return, not even thanks. It never seeks to know what its results are. It just gives and flows, and comes back to give and flow endlessly.

The advantages of nuclear therapy become more evident as we use it. We realize that we are coming into a recognition of Christian fellowship, which I have the courage to call "spiritual communism". This day we can dedicate ourselves to a great dynamic movement of spiritual communism. If anything is going to counteract the material communism it must be from the spirit.

Many wonderful principles are born out of a fellowship of dedication, as well as out of sorrow and suffering. Out of the French people came the lofty principles of equality, fraternity and liberty, which rose in the hearts of a great people who had suffered and were reaching out for the deeper verities of life. It swept the masses like a great religious revival, but they forgot to put God at the head of their movement as they should have done if they expected the spearhead to go forward into the future to build permanently into a new pattern.

Because they forgot God, their ideas of equality, fraternity, and liberty leaped across the Atlantic and came to birth in another continent. It came into America and bore its fruit, because our forefathers, in prayer, dedicated the whole movement to God, and dared to put "In God we trust" on the face of the coins which were to pass under their hands each day.

Is history repeating itself before our eyes? Are we seeing the same thing happening in our own day? The movement in Russia arising in the hearts of another great people who had suffered much and were reaching out for the deeper verities of life, struck fire again in the idea of sacrifice of the individual for the sake of the group. But they, too, forgot that no movement can go forward to fulfilment without divine guidance. They, too, left out God.

May history again repeat itself, and that great movement leap across another sea into another continent, and come to fruition in Japan or India, where other millions, having been humbled through suffering, are willing to put God in the forefront of their government and their lives. The principles of democracy united with the Christ-principle of selflessness is the emerging ideology of the new age. Many believe that group therapy which is being developed has far deeper significance than appears on the surface.

* * *

Though we practise nuclear therapy, we grant that the personal interview is sometimes both important and necessary. Under the pattern habit of repeating a life-story there often lies another story which is never faced until an inner conviction, a desire for release, or the observation of others and praying for their needs, brings it to the surface. It is a tremendous thing when it comes.

It cannot happen often. It is a true catharsis of the soul, in which we bare our innermost selves and stand naked before God. Adam and Eve are pictured standing in the garden of Eden naked before the Lord because you cannot cover yourself when you stand before Him. No alibis can clothe you. There can be nothing between you and your Maker. Nothing can remain hidden in you. You must jettison everything.

So while we grant that the personal interview is sometimes important and necessary, we realize that the pattern habit carried over from years of consultation with medical doctors and religious teachers is something that must be changed. What many fail to realize is that the constant repetition of a negative picture drives it all more firmly into the subconscious mind. At Merrybrook we became aware that this pattern must be broken down. We sought direction through prayer. Perhaps I can tell you the answer by telling you the story of Harriet.

Harriet came to us with all the outward appearance of problems, spiritual, physical and mental. She was a beautiful woman, but she was quite evidently carrying a heavy burden. In the evening, after her arrival, she made the usual request, "How soon can I have a personal talk with you? There are so many things I want to tell you." We walked out arm in arm through those lovely grounds, under the great maple trees, and we said to Harriet, "We see that you are carrying many problems; that you suffer from tensions and perhaps from high blood pressure.

"You have come here seeking rest and spiritual renewal. You would like to go away with all these things behind you. You want peace of mind and healing of body before you leave us. But if you tell us all the old problems, and insist upon painting a picture in our consciousness of the negative side of your life, do you realize that we are going to have to erase that picture before we can help you make another of what you want to be? You want our best for you. Will you help us by not fixing in our consciousness a picture which we would have to erase?"

There was a hedge in front of us. "Do you see this barberry hedge?" we asked her. "Would you like to take all the negative things you have wanted to tell us about, all the problems you have been carrying so long, all the burdens you brought up here with you, put them all into an imaginary bundle and throw them behind the hedge? If you will do this, then we three will have a blank page on which to make a new picture. We can then help you to build a new life. We can help to rename your world."

Harriet caught the idea immediately.

No one could have been more responsive. As the days passed we saw her burdens fall away and her tensions relaxing. All signs of indigestion disappeared. She moved with ease, and even ran up and down the steps, her stiff joints forgotten.

* * *

Nuclear therapy has other salient points to recommend it. Each one in the group is a channel through which the healing-power may flow to someone whose need is as great or greater than their own. This cosmic power is not to be received and retained. It is a power which you take in and immediately pass on. If it does not flow it is not alive.

The living power flowing through you gives you more life, but to be dynamic it must constantly be given out. You who would find your life must lose it. St. John saw it as the divine circulation and described it as a great river of life coming out of the heart of God, flowing into the hearts of man, and flowing back again into the heart of God. It must be a continuous flow.

That is why we need to learn to be less and less conscious of ourselves. In the Camps Farthest Out we have daily rhythms to help us release ourselves, and become less self-conscious. Classes in writing, painting and music are designed to give us this release of self in creative expression. In nuclear therapy we think less and less of our individual needs or problems and more and more about our oneness with other people.

We pray not so much that God take away sickness, sorrow, hurt or want, as we pray that we may be lifted up into the consciousness which was in Christ Jesus. We pray not so much that God may grant this desire or that, but that we may be lifted up into the fullness of His presence, for in that Presence illness and hurt fall into nothingness and all God's substance flows toward us to fill our every need.

As we work and pray together daily we come to recognize that we have one common problem. We have only one. All others stem from this, and that problem is how to realize God—how to live in the Presence of Jesus Christ.

The details of the problem do not matter at all. It may be psychological, spiritual or physical; it may be a hardened liver, a broken heart or incompatibility with those nearest to you. It doesn't make any difference. It is all one. It is your problem. To you it is important and vital. To you it seems that everyone should listen to it, but after just a little reflection you realize that each one who is in the group also has a problem. To every one their problem is important and vital and should be listened to. So you merge your problem with another's. You take on the problem of another, forgetting your own. This is true spiritual therapy, and this is spiritual communism.

The result is that you find your own problem becoming smaller and smaller as your desire to help others becomes greater and greater. You find that it is true that he who loses his life shall find it.

When two or three are gathered together in His name a prayer cell is formed. There may be readings, audible and silent prayer, but the most important principle to be followed is complete forgetfulness of self in concern for the needs of others. In your prayer-groups it would be well to say, "You need not tell us about your problems, but bring the innermost secrets of your heart and tell them to God. Tell them only to Him."

Then, as you come together week after week, praying for the needs of others, you will feel the problems of the others in the group, and you will become more and more open to them. As you become more conscious of the love of God in your own life, project that love to another as you would project a beam of light. Thus you share the suffering of others constructively. This is the lesson of the cross.

"Intercessory prayer," as Bishop Charles H. Brent has said, "is not scattering good wishes in the air toward someone we desire to serve. Neither is it the vocal or silent utterance of pious hopes in the direction of God.

"It is the orderly operation of a vital energy; an immediate transmitting of life, where the person prayed for is actively receptive, and the creation of fresh opportunity for him, whatever his temper of mind.

"By the force of spiritual projection which eliminates space by ignoring it, we lay our lives over against those of our friends, simultaneously establishing definite and conscious contact with God. . . . Our lives become open for God's use in the bestowal of His gifts. We become agents of power for others.

"God's strength, God's love, God's healing life flow through us to others. Thus prayer takes on a new and inspiring meaning."

Being still and listening you will be given the perfect word for each one's condition. Attuning your ear to the voice of

Spirit, you will receive the highest wisdom—even the word of Truth itself. Abide in that word; let it abide in you, and the one you pray for will hear it also. "He will walk in the light and the glory of Sonship will shine in him."

"I will instruct thee and teach thee" is the promise. "I will show thee great and mighty things which thou knowest not . . . I will lead thee in paths thou hast not known."

THE END

Two other vital books complete Dr. Rebecca Beard's famous HEALING TRILOGY. The reader is invited to obtain EVERYMAN'S GOAL, price 95p, *post* 10p, *and EVERYMAN'S MISSION, price* 95p, *post* 10p. *Copies of Dr. Beard's books can be obtained from bookshops or by return post from the publishers,*

ARTHUR JAMES LTD., THE DRIFT, EVESHAM, WORCS.